Advanced
SAT, ACT, LSAT, GMAT

REALTIME

VOCABULARY WORKBOOK

M. Monette Benoit, B. B.A., Paralegal;
Tutor, Career Coach, Consultant; CART Captioner;
CCR, Certified Court Reporter;
CRI, Certified Reporting Instructor;
CPE, Certified Program Evaluator;
Author; Public Speaker; Columnist;
Contributing Editor, NCRA, National Court Reporters Association,
JCR, Journal of Court Reporting

All American RealTime/Captioning Services, Inc.
ARTCS.com

–and–

Emmett J. Donnelly, B.S., English, Languages, and Science Majors; M. Ed.;
Guidance Counselor; Psychologist; Social Worker;
Academician; Researcher; and Historian

THIRD EDITION by Monette Benoit

Copyright with updates © 2021 - 1993

Court Reporter Reference Books & CDs
CRRbooks.com

Blog: *Monette's Musings & Monette's Mindful Management*
www.monettebenoit.com

Those that do not read are condemned to live but one life. –Anonymous

© Monette Benoit

CRRbooks.com

Court Reporting Whispere

© Tutoring & Coaching

A powerful agent is the right word.

Whenever we come upon
one of those intensely right words
the resulting effect is physical
as well as spiritual,
and electrically prompt.
–Mark Twain

Visit our web site for products, services, free articles: www.CRRbooks.com

THIRD EDITION

Copyright with updates © 2021 - 1993 by Monette Benoit

ISBN   1-881149-02-1
PRINTED IN THE UNITED STATES OF AMERICA

The Symptoms of Inner Peace

A tendency to think and act spontaneously from fears
based on past experiences; an unmistakable ability to enjoy each moment;
a loss of interest in judging others; a loss of interest in judging self;
a loss of interest in conflict;
a loss of interest in interpreting the actions of others;
a loss of ability to worry; frequent attacks of smiling through the heart;
increasing susceptibility to love extended by others,
as well as the uncontrollable urge to extend it;
an increasing tendency to let things happen,
rather than to manipulate them and to make them happen.
–Author Unknown

This *Workbook* is dedicated to wise individuals each sharing inner peace:

Judy Larson, CRI, Real-Time Instructor,
St. Louis Community College at Meramac, St. Louis, Missouri;

David Langford, RMR, CRR, CSR, Official Real-Time Reporter,
Computer-Integrated Courtroom, Dallas, Texas;

Judy and David encouraged me, shared expertise, love, and wisdom.
They helped me to laugh at myself and comforted me while I was on this journey.
Each shared a wonderful friendship, and I thank you.
You changed my world, Judy and David.

And
Captain Kevin Drue Donnelly, U.S. Army,
Author, *The Panama Story*
Available free on the Internet: www.captainkevindonnelly.com
deceased August 5th, 2000, with HCV, Hepatitis C.

My brave brother Captain Kevin comforted, researched, educated, and
guided soldiers, veterans, vet spouses, children, siblings, friends,
his parents, and strangers to a life … and sadly, many to a death …
with dignity and respect. *"Why*? I gave him my Word."

Additional information may be found: www.captainkevindonnelly.com

Tutoring and Coaching / Monette Benoit

The **NCRA CBC and CCP Textbook** is now available from CRRbooks.com.

** <u>Fact</u>: Television stations are now requiring captioners to provide their CBC (Certified Broadcast Captioner) certification to receive captioning work due to quality standard regulations that went into effect January 15, 2015.

** <u>Fact</u>: Many employers now require the CCP (Certified CART Provider) certification for educational CART and CART venues.

** <u>Fact</u>: Many courts and firms now give financial incentive for additional certification.

** <u>Fact</u>: I desire to serve you. Always have. Always will. This is my mission.

Many instructors, court reporters, CART Captioners, and students have endorsed <u>Court Reporter Reference</u> products. A partial listing on www.CRRbooks.com includes:

Mary Smith Agren, RPR, CRI, FAPR; Martin H. Block, RPR, FAPR; Jack Boenau, RDR, CRR, CBC, CCP; Judith Brentano, RPR, FAPR; Robert Clark, NCRA Librarian-Historian; Kevin Wm. Daniel, RDR, CRR, CBC, CCP, FAPR (Author, *Writing Naked*); Kathy DiLorenzo, RDR, CRR, CBC, FAPR; Steve Edmondson, CLVS; Joshua Foley, CCP; Gayl Hardeman, RDR, CRR, CCP, FAPR (Author, *De~Puzz~Ler Essential Dictionary Makeover*); Cheryl Hoover; Suzanne Small Kelly, RDR, CRR, CBC, CPE; Mary Knapp, RPR, FAPR (Author, *Legal Terminology* and *The Complete Court Reporter's Handbook*); Judy Larson; Richard Lederer, NCRA Language Columnist, Ph.D.; Jean Melone, CRI; Pauletta Morse, Ph.D., CRI; Robert McCormick, Ph.D., CRI, Ms. Ed., (Author, RealWrite/RealTime Theory); Jan McNally, Ph.D.; Eleanor Mitchell, RPR; Nancy Patterson, RPR, CRI, FAPR (Author, *Preparing for the RPR, CM Written Knowledge Test*); Anita Paul, RPR, CRR, CBC, CCP, CRI, CPE, Realtime Seminars; Sarah Prince; Kathy Robson, RPR, CRR, CBC; Beverly Ritter, StenEd Educational Products; Jennifer Sati, RMR, CRR, CBC, CCP, CRI; Alison Selfridge, RDR, CRI; Sheryl Stapp, RPR; Carol Thomas, RPR; Ed Varallo, RMR, CRR, FAPR (Author, *The Real-Time Writer's Manual*); Rhonda M. Zacharias, RPR, CRR, CRI, RMR, FAPR; Lynne Marie Zakrzewski, RMR, CRR, CBC, CPE; and instructors, CART Captioners, court reporters, and students who find the material organized and easy to understand within the U.S. and 17 countries.

TABLE OF CONTENTS

> ****Pedagogically sound covering a wealth of material
> with facts, tips, information. Time-Tested, Proven
> In the Classroom and Independent Study****

The world's largest library of *court reporter training, *private tutoring, *career coaching, *test prep!

Complete NCRA and State RPR, RDR, CSR WKT Test Prep Textbook, 6th Edition, Updated/Revised

<u>2015 Sixth Edition</u> *Textbook*: Only textbook on the market! Latin, legal, court terms; detailed grammar, punctuation; vocabulary; medical; Expanded **Test-Taking Tips; **Additional Focus Tips; ** Updated/Expanded Computer Terminology, **Technology, **Advisory Opinions, **Ethics

Workbook follows the *Complete WKT Text*: <u>testing resource</u> with Latin, legal, court terms; grammar; vocabulary; medical; computer sections -- <u>**approximately 2,002 practice test questions**</u>

Companion Workbook Study Guide follows the *Workbook*, cross-referencing each word, showing where and how words are used. Learn why an answer is correct, incorrect, or the distracting answer

** "Test Prep Set" – four-volume set – is CRRbooks.com's bestseller consisting of the *Complete WKT Textbook, Workbook, Companion Study Guide,* and *Realtime Vocabulary Workbook* **

Vastly improve skills for greater career opportunities with CART Captioning and court reporting.

---

*Learn *How* to Test. ** Pass the first time!

Join the thousands of students, novice and long-time professionals who have discovered:
- The highest-result NCRA and State Test Prep Textbook and Workbooks for testing success;
- Affordable tutoring and confidential one-on-one private coaching for your accelerated progress;
- Simple time-management and organized motivational skills to keep you moving forward.

*Are you struggling with tests, motivation, personal challenges, focus, and/or speedbuilding?

Veteran court reporter, Monette Benoit, multiple-title author of books and test prep for the CART Captioning and reporting industry helps clients achieve at higher levels. Build new strengths in testing, focus, and speedbuilding. **Email <u>Monette@CRRbooks.com</u> about <u>tutoring</u>, <u>coaching packages</u>.**

Nationally known as the *Court Reporting Whisperer*, Monette provides tutoring and career coaching.

Get the latest tips and advice from **www.monettebenoit.com** and **www.CRRbooks.com**
"Monette's Musings" contains information for busy professionals and students.

**NEW: RealTime Dictionary Builder, <u>www.realtimedictionarybuilder.com</u>
Championed by Kathy DiSanti DiLorenzo, RDR-CRR-CBC, and many others.**

As a student, I felt inclined to study this material as I did academic tests. Much of the material reviewed appeared on the exam. **This text is a wonderful tool** that should be utilized by students and reporters everywhere as an aid in passing written tests. **– Laura Ballard, RPR, CSR – Ex-Student**

Having been a captioner and out of reporting and testing arenas, I knew I would cram for the NCRA RDR, Registered Diplomate Reporter, exam. I chose **this textbook** and the <u>REALTIME Vocabulary Workbook</u> to bring myself up to date – and how out of date I was! **These books have excellent study material for the CSR, RPR, and RMR.** I received my RDR results. Thanks, Monette! **– Kathy DiSanti DiLorenzo, *RDR-CRR-CBC***

To join our successful ranks, go to: <u>www.CRRbooks.com</u>

PREFACE

WANTED:

PERSONS WILLING TO LEARN and EXPAND THEIR KNOWLEDGE

**Out of 615,000 words currently in the English language,
How many words have you used this year – or today?**

French has approximately only 100,000 words. Since English has so many words, an estimated 615,000, English presents challenges to students who need academic testing, are preparing for standardized tests, and to professionals who communicate and work in realtime. The *REALTIME Vocabulary Workbook* will cultivate and expand your vocabulary knowledge.

This workbook is different from other vocabulary books; the lessons are designed to be self-taught. **Each section has two answer keys and requires a dictionary and a thesaurus**, a combination guaranteed to increase and catapult your skills! You will reduce your fatigue factor and improve your comprehensibility with customized material contained in this book.

Students and adults need to be able to instantly recognize words. With continued advancements in technology, when a person composes email and uses social media to post or tweet, readers now form judgments about that person and their vocabulary.

Professional occupations necessitate high vocabulary skills. For example, court reporters and CART Captioners now write "in realtime" instantly producing words. We use technology that enables each person to strike a word on the stenotype keyboard. That word is immediately searched in the reporter's computer dictionary matching the steno strokes and English translation. Within seconds, an English translation occurs on the computer, monitor, or television screen. Individuals who benefit from our realtime skills include deaf and hearing-impaired, English as a second language, attention deficit, learning disabled, and brained-injured children and adults.

i

The ADA mandates that all individuals receive equal access in communication. Realtime and elevated vocabulary skills raise 'the bar' for *all* people.

Mistakes now are viewed almost immediately by people who watch streaming text and read tweets and posts on social media sites. This demand for a thorough vocabulary reflects advances in our technology that is continuing to expand and for **all academic standardized tests**.

This *REALTIME Vocabulary Workbook* has been specifically designed with varied exercises to increase skills, to advance professional and personal performance, to hold the reader's attention, and to make the learning process enjoyable. Learning should be fun and not boring. The varied chapters and sections will assist each reader to focus, expediting the learning process!

Everyone has two vocabulary levels: a speaking vocabulary and a reading vocabulary. Normally, a reading vocabulary is higher than the speaking vocabulary.

New words represent new experiences, new travels. They are symbols of items, objects, thoughts, or memories. Every time you learn a word, you build a world, create an experience, and capture a moment in time.

Words, like songs and great art, evoke feelings, and create memories.

Words represent who we are in life. How rich in experiences do you want to be?

Pull up a chair. Come share new experiences and moments with the *REALTIME Vocabulary Workbook.*

Knowledge is the true organ of sight, not the eyes. –Panchatantra

*When you look into a mirror you do not see your reflection,
your reflection sees you.*   –Anonymous

INTRODUCTION

Monette Benoit was awarded an Associate Degree in court reporting by the State University of New York at Alfred in 1976. She completed an undergraduate paralegal program at Adelphi University in 1979. She has worked as a court reporter and paralegal. In 1989 she returned to the field of court reporting education and began teaching Legal Terminology, Courtroom Procedures, speedbuilding, and a Written Knowledge Test prep course she developed. She earned her CRI (Certified Reporting Instructor) certification from the NCRA, National Court Reporters Association, in 1992. In 1993 she earned her Bachelor of Business Administration at Northwood University, and in 1995 she earned the CPE (Certified Program Evaluator) from the NCRA. She has been employed as a judicial and freelance court reporter, CART Captioner, instructor, consultant, grant writer, author, tutor, life coach, and international speaker.

Currently, this vocabulary workbook is used by high school students; college, law school, and graduate degree applicants, and civil service candidates.

The *Associated Press Stylebook and Libel Manual, American Heritage Dictionary* and *A Manual of Style, Prepared by the U.S. Government Printing Office* were used as expert references. A complete list of reference material is listed in the bibliography.

The *Advanced SAT, ACT, LSAT, GMAT REALTIME Vocabulary Workbook* was initially created to supplement the *Complete NCRA RPR, RDR, state CSR WKT Test Prep Textbook; WKT Test Prep Workbook*; and *Companion Study Guide* for court reporters, CART Captioners, and students for national and state court reporting boards.

The Preface details further information.

Emmett James Donnelly graduated from Fordham University and attended Fordham College of Education studying psychology, philosophy, Latin, Greek, German, and chemistry. He completed his Master of Education degree at the University of Houston studying counseling and English literature.

Mr. Donnelly worked as a psychiatric social worker in an Army hospital before working as a social worker supervising foster children placements. He was employed as a veteran's education advisor prior to becoming a high school teacher in the Houston public school system, working with students who had dropped out of school. In New York, Emmett Donnelly taught junior high school English, science, math, and chemistry before becoming a guidance counselor and continuing his pursuit towards his doctorate. For eight years he was in charge of the school system's education records and college recommendations while serving as registrar. Mr. Donnelly continued to teach, counsel, and also taught high school equivalency classes to adults preparing for federal and state civil service examinations.

Emmett Donnelly retired after thirty-one years with the same school district, and currently travels the country with his wife researching new books.

Monette Benoit has been a speaker at many state court reporting association conventions; NCRA court reporting, NCRA student, and NCRA teaching conventions; and she was keynote speaker in Fremantle, Australia, and Edmonton, Canada. Her products are used by professionals in 17 countries. Monette has worked with students, CART Captioners, novice and experienced court reporters preparing for national RPR, RMR, RDR, CRR, CCP, CBC, and state certifications. In addition, she has published and marketed through her company, CRR Books & CDs, educational products, the *Realtime Dictionary Builder* series, multiple products, and tutoring services to assist students, onsite and remote CART Captioners, and judicial and freelance reporters.

Many television stations now require the CBC (Certified Broadcast Captioner) and the CRR (Certified Realtime Reporter) **certificate** for each captioner to be on file with the station because higher quality standard regulations, required by law, are effective January 15, 2015.

Many employers are now requiring the CCP (Certified CART Provider) **certificate** for CART employment, including educational CART.

Monette Benoit's *Complete NCRA CBC and CCP Written Test Prep Textbook* is available to assist CART Captioners to pass this milestone and to meet employer's and station's certification qualifications.

iv

The website CRRbooks.com lists the expanding product line to also include the Realtime Dictionary Builder. This product is a tool for students, court reporters, and CART Captioners using powerful dictionary-building topics and the ever-continuing, mandatory dictionary maintenance.

Monette's goal is to help you to remember to write each word efficiently, accurately, without hesitation. She is honored to continue to assist you, as she has since 1988.

The Realtime Required Primer bundle consists of four academic products:

1) *Complete NCRA RPR, RDR, and State CSR WKT Prep Textbook;*
2) *WKT Test Prep Workbook;*
3) *WKT Test Prep Companion Study Guide;* and
4) *REALTIME Vocabulary Workbook.*

Monette's Musings, a blog, contains articles written by Monette for her NCRA *JCR, Journal of Court Reporting,* columns: *Beyond The Comfort Zone, Ask The Coach,* and *Coach's Corner.* Topics include motivation, testing tips, advice for students, CART FAQ, working with sign interpreters, working with Deaf and hard-of-hearing consumers, realtime writing, challenging moments, humor, historical events, and much more.

Monette Benoit formed The A.R.T.S., The American RealTime/Captioning Services, in 1993. ARTCS.com lists additional details. She lectures, consults, and mentors with universities, community colleges, business institutions, private entities, religious groups, student disabled service managers, human resource departments, independent living services, CART Captioners, and judicial and freelance court reporters.

She's a motivational speaker on technology and education, inspiring reporters and students at state court reporting associations' annual conventions, national reporting conventions, meetings, and within classrooms. Monette discusses assistive technology and CART Captioning as they relate to working with individuals challenged by attention deficit syndrome, learning disabilities, brain-injuries, English as a second language, special education, spinal cord injuries, and arenas outside legal settings.

She has consulted with authors completing educational publications and has contributed information for chapters on assistive technology to a special education textbook currently distributed nationally to adult students in special education in university curricula. Additionally, she developed a CART and captioning curriculum for an NCRA-endorsed state university using federal grant money.

Monette provides CART Captioning of religious services, baptisms, funerals; international, national, and local conventions; seminars; meetings; class lectures; PTA meetings; technology gatherings; defensive driving classes; HLAA (formerly SHHH) meetings; and independent living service meetings for children, teens, adults, and senior citizens who are deaf and hard-of-hearing. She works side by side with sign interpreters for Deaf and HOH events and consults with onsite and remote sign interpreters building teams for total access to communication.

The *WKT Test Prep Workbook* and *WKT Test Prep Companion Study Guide* were created to supplement the *Revised/Updated Complete NCRA RPR, RDR, and State CSR WKT Test Prep Textbook.*

Each book is practical when the exercises in each chapter are used to test learning objectives to pass a test, to write realtime, and to advance skills. Individuals pass NCRA and state written knowledge tests with a 98% successful pass rate the first time when CRR Books are used as a primary review source.

Welcome, adult learner. We salute your quest to improve your knowledge and education. Monette continues to listen to you and to your requests.

You can find details about products and services with the Court Reporting Whisperer, Monette Benoit, at www.CRRbooks.com.

You can preach a better sermon with your life than with your lips. –Oliver Goldsmith

Dear God, I pray for patience. And I want it right now!"   –Oren Arnold

INSTRUCTIONS

This book is practical when the information in each chapter is used to test learning objectives.

The *REALTIME Vocabulary Workbook* is designed to be used with a thesaurus and a dictionary to increase vocabulary. The vocabulary workbook has two answer keys and is a necessity in building vocabulary mechanics

TEACHER'S INSTRUCTIONS

You may assign the *Vocabulary Workbook* in an English class; SAT, ACT, GMAT, LSAT, or GRE study group. Plus, you now have material for any vocabulary class and for this important evaluation.

You should instruct your students not to memorize the material, but to understand and to learn from exercises in each book.

COURSE OBJECTIVES

After completing The *Advanced SAT, ACT, LSAT, GMAT REALTIME Vocabulary Workbook* your students will be able to:

1. Evaluate comparisons, sequences, outcomes, assess, and detail relevant information.

2. Spell and define word mechanics, roots of words, as well as prefixes, suffixes, and information.

3. Analyze and distinguish vocabulary words and hyphenation word divisions.

4. Identify and define words that are misspelled, abbreviated, and misdefined.

5. Describe differences between misspelled words, compound words, plural words, spelling errors, and unrelated word groupings.

6. List examples of antonyms, synonyms, eponyms, and grammatical sentences.

7. Form sentences from words listed in each chapter.

8. Research and introduce new vocabulary and definitions into their recognition vocabulary.

9. Demonstrate knowledge to receive a passing grade on quizzes preparing for a test.

10. Increase vocabulary of all listed words, foreign words, and phrases.

11. Identify areas that may be weak and need improvement.

GRADING

A letter grade, percentage scores, or a pass/fail credit may be assigned.

The grading for your class of students or adult learners should be higher than the grade required on your SAT, ACT, state regents, GMAT, LSAT, and GRE.

I want to thank the instructors who have taken time to review, offer suggestions, and to respond with information that has been used to improve my products.

> May you get all your wishes but one,
> So you always have something to strive for.
> –Irish Blessing

> We grow neither better nor worse as we get old,
> But more like ourselves.   –Mary Lamberton Becker

> Unless we try to do something beyond what we have
> Already mastered, we cannot grow.   –Ronald Osborn

> Tell me something and I'll forget it. Show me something and I'll remember it.
> Involve me in something and I'll understand it.   –Chinese Proverb

STUDENT'S / PROFESSIONAL'S INSTRUCTIONS

Welcome. You are about to begin a new chapter in your life. This study time will prepare you for academics, scholastic written tests, and for a professional career. The Preface and Introduction in this workbook contain valuable information to assist you.

If you are studying independently, read the directions to each exercise carefully.

Be sure to use a dictionary and a thesaurus with each section to guarantee increasing your vocabulary. The dictionary and thesaurus reference material used with each section of this workbook will further explain information for this book and expedite the learning process.   If you are preparing for the SAT, ACT, LSAT, GMAT, or GRE, you now have material to test multi-skilled levels for this important evaluation. The exercises in the chapters are designed to increase your skills in each area where you are expected to be tested.

You can improve your studies and knowledge, and actually look forward to using your new skills to pass the important test. Set aside a time to study, create a body of knowledge from which to study, and then just study!

All information is in quiz format. All answers **in two answer keys** are listed in the back so that you can check on your progress. I instruct my students to write in your book and use it as their personal study tool.

The entertainment and encouragement in the poetry located throughout this book was included to inspire you, help you to smile, and to relieve stress.   You will have comprehensive information to evaluate your strengths and weaknesses, to study, drill, quiz, review, and to reinforce material.

It was the bumble bee and the butterfly that survived,
Not the dinosaurs. —Meridel Le Suer

Do not memorize the words on each page. Read and review each page until you understand each page fully before moving ahead. Work on one chapter a time. Do not jump around and skip sections without completing the entire chapter. You will enhance your study time when you understand and master one area before embarking on another chapter.

Write the words you are studying in this workbook, in a notebook, or on index cards. Review these words throughout the day. Study the definitions and words given in each chapter. Such material should be reviewed regularly to ensure retention.

Review, review, review, and continue to study this information until you can read each page – read each page – anticipating and knowing the correct term, definition, and answer.

Compile your reference books in a specific study area as you work on each chapter. Thirty minutes of thorough, comprehensive study is better than one hour of distracted searches for the correct definition and/or explanation.

The unique books, CDs, and products at RealtimeDictionaryBuilder.com were prepared by Monette Benoit, a court reporter, realtime writer, CART Provider, captioner, teacher, motivational speaker, grant writer, NCRA *JCR* contributing editor, tutor, life coach, private consultant, and author.

Welcome! Monette Benoit has been waiting for you! Now, let's begin together.

Sow a thought, you reap desire.
Sow a desire, you reap a habit.
So a habit, you reap a character.
So a character, you reap your destiny.
–Author Unknown

CHAPTER 1: VOCABULARY BUILDING

Roots, Prefixes, Suffixes

Fill in the first blank with the number of the correct matching term. Write a word which contains the numbered prefix, suffix, or root in the space provided. Words with roots, prefixes and suffixes are listed in Answer Key #2.

Section One

1. extra	a. ____	quality or state	1. _____
2. anthro	b. ____	prior to	_____
3. scrip	c. ____	to send	_____
4. ver	d. ____	good	_____
5. mis	e. ____	human	_____
6. re	f. ____	beyond	_____
7. pro	g. ____	truth	_____
8. hetero	h. ____	write	_____
9. ency	i. ____	different	_____
10. eu	j. ____	again	_____

Section Two

11. mal	a. ____	around	11. _____
12. post	b. ____	without	_____
13. pro	c. ____	away from	_____
14. chron	d. ____	bad	_____
15. a	e. ____	to wander	_____
16. hyper	f. ____	after	_____
17. err	g. ____	end	_____
18. peri	h. ____	time	_____
19. fin	i. ____	excessive	_____
20. dis	j. ____	for	_____

Section Three

21. ab	a. ____	life	21. _____
22. be	b. ____	hear	_____
23. fore	c. ____	all	_____
24. vi	d. ____	away from	_____
25. ped	e. ____	similar	_____
26. di	f. ____	to have certain quality	_____
27. par	g. ____	to fight	_____
28. aud	h. ____	before	_____
29. pug	i. ____	apart	_____
30. omni	j. ____	child	_____

1©

Section Four

31.	am	a. ____	against	31. _____
32.	bi	b. ____	akin to	_____
33.	co	c. ____	big	_____
34.	ish	d. ____	love	_____
35.	dia	e. ____	on all sides	_____
36.	sci	f. ____	together	_____
37.	circu	g. ____	out of	_____
38.	ant	h. ____	through	_____
39.	e	i. ____	twice	_____
40.	mag	j. ____	to know	_____

Section Five

41.	intra	a. ____	mixed	41. _____
42.	ver	b. ____	small	_____
43.	arch	c. ____	toward	_____
44.	ad	d. ____	across	_____
45.	inter	e. ____	within	_____
46.	min	f. ____	completely	_____
47.	sup	g. ____	turn	_____
48.	trans	h. ____	chief	_____
49.	per	i. ____	below	_____
50.	misc	j. ____	between	_____

Section Six

51.	ped	a. ____	before	51. _____
52.	infra	b. ____	self	_____
53.	hydr	c. ____	foot	_____
54.	art	d. ____	same	_____
55.	ante	e. ____	beneath	_____
56.	pre	f. ____	shape	_____
57.	de	g. ____	skill	_____
58.	hom	h. ____	reversal	_____
59.	morph	i. ____	water	_____
60.	auto	j. ____	before	_____

Love thy neighbor as thyself, but choose your neighborhood.
—Louise Beal

Section Seven

61. ery	a. ____ throw	61. _____
62. cip	b. ____ among, with, change	_____
63. sol	c. ____ qualities collectively	_____
64. tract	d. ____ to lead	_____
65. ous	e. ____ take	_____
66. port	f. ____ stand	_____
67. ject	g. ____ pull	_____
68. duct	h. ____ carry	_____
69. sist	i. ____ loosen	_____
70. meta	j. ____ full of	_____

Section Eight

71. vis	a. ____ harm	71. _____
72. rog	b. ____ grow	_____
73. nox	c. ____ see	_____
74. fid	d. ____ take	_____
75. dict	e. ____ ask	_____
76. jur	f. ____ fire	_____
77. fer	g. ____ trust	_____
78. cre	h. ____ law	_____
79. pyr	i. ____ tell	_____
80. cept	j. ____ bring	_____

Section Nine

81. amb	a. ____ above	81. _____
82. ben	b. ____ many	_____
83. dom	c. ____ other	_____
84. sur	d. ____ good	_____
85. im	e. ____ love	_____
86. ex	f. ____ both	_____
87. al	g. ____ around	_____
88. circu	h. ____ into	_____
89. phil	i. ____ out of	_____
90. poly	j. ____ quality of	_____

Death is not the greatest loss in life.
The greatest loss is what dies inside us while we live.
—Norman Cousins

3 ©

© Tutoring & Coaching

Section Ten

91.	ob	a. ____	one's own	91. _____
92.	neo	b. ____	everywhere	_____
93.	pen	c. ____	toward	_____
94.	man	d. ____	alongside	_____
95.	hypo	e. ____	new	_____
96.	id	f. ____	to make	_____
97.	gen	g. ____	hand	_____
98.	pan	h. ____	to pay	_____
99.	for	i. ____	birth	_____
100.	para	j. ____	under	_____

Section Eleven

101.	un	a. ____	cause	101. _____
102.	ly	b. ____	permit	_____
103.	oid	c. ____	condition	_____
104.	ism	d. ____	nature of	_____
105.	oper	e. ____	upon	_____
106.	ate	f. ____	resembling	_____
107.	dyn	g. ____	not	_____
108.	ine	h. ____	work	_____
109.	epi	i. ____	like	_____
110.	lic	j. ____	power	_____

Section Twelve

111.	il	a. ____	first	111. _____
112.	soph	b. ____	please	_____
113.	bene	c. ____	light	_____
114.	apo	d. ____	upon	_____
115.	hum	e. ____	wash	_____
116.	prim	f. ____	earth	_____
117.	luc	g. ____	wisdom	_____
118.	sume	h. ____	away from	_____
119.	lav	i. ____	good	_____
120.	plac	j. ____	take	_____

God grant me the serenity
To accept the things I cannot change;
The courage to change the things I can;
And the wisdom to know the difference.
—Reinhold Niebuhr

Similar Suffixes

Fill in the blanks with the number of the matching word.

Section One   People who study...

1. otologist   a. ____ women's diseases
2. rhinologist   b. ____ glands of internal secretion
3. ophthalmologist   c. ____ fossils
4. endocrinologist   d. ____ ears
5. psychologist   e. ____ old age
6. entomologist   f. ____ eyes
7. gynecologist   g. ____ birds
8. ornithologist   h. ____ human mind and behavior
9. paleontologist   i. ____ noses
10. gerontologist   j. ____ insects

Section Two   People who study...

11. seismologist   a. ____ former history through material
                                         remains
12. neurologist   b. ____ poisons
13. etymologist   c. ____ earthquakes
14. archaeologist   d. ____ heart
15. pathologist   e. ____ origin of words
16. speleologist   f. ____ snakes
17. cardiologist   g. ____ nature and origin of disease
18. toxicologist   h. ____ caves
19. dermatologist   i. ____ skin
20. herpetologist   j. ____ nerves

Section Three   The study of...

21. chronology   a. ____ languages, linguistics
22. horology   b. ____ secret codes
23. embryology   c. ____ the development of man
24. cryptology   d. ____ structure of cells
25. theology   e. ____ the determination of dates
26. cytology   f. ____ tissues under a microscope
27. philology   g. ____ organisms in early stages of
                                         development
28. histology   h. ____ religion, nature of God
29. geology   i. ____ timepieces
30. anthropology   j. ____ the earth as recorded in its rocks

Section Four   The study of...

  31. ontology   a. ____ relationship between organisms
                                                   and their environment
  32. ethology   b. ____ fresh water organisms and
                                                   phenomena
  33. pedology   c. ____ trees
  34. oology   d. ____ the universe
  35. dendrology   e. ____ animal behavior
  36. ethnology   f. ____ fungi
  37. limnology   g. ____ birds' eggs
  38. cosmology   h. ____ soils
  39. mycology   i. ____ the races of mankind
  40. ecology   j. ____ being and existence (philosophy)

Section Five   The study of...

  41. graphology   a. ____ causes of natural phenomena,
                                                  for example, diseases
  42. pharmacology   b. ____ tumors
  43. meteorology   c. ____ digestive tract
  44. morphology   d. ____ handwriting
  45. traumatology   e. ____ loss of physical sensation
  46. etiology   f. ____ weather
  47. topology   g. ____ drugs
  48. gastroenterology   h. ____ wounds, injuries
  49. anesthesiology   i. ____ geometric configurations
  50. oncology   j. ____ form and structure of living
                                                  organisms

Section Six   The study of...

  51. petrology   a. ____ phenomena not explained by
                                                  known natural laws
  52. sociology   b. ____ the nature of being (philosophy)
  53. parapsychology   c. ____ prison management
  54. epistemology   d. ____ water
  55. penology   e. ____ death and mourning
  56. osteology   f. ____ origin and composition of rocks
  57. ontology   g. ____ parasitism
  58. thanatology   h. ____ human social behavior
  59. parasitology   i. ____ bones
  60. hydrology   j. ____ nature and theory of knowledge

6 ©

Section Seven

The study and science of...

61. cryogenics
62. epigraphy
63. historiography
64. orthography

65. pedagogy
66. demography
67. lexography
68. cartography
69. chromatography
70. lithology

a. ____ dictionaries and words
b. ____ teaching
c. ____ maps
d. ____ mineral composition and structure of rocks
e. ____ chemical analysis of a mixture
f. ____ correct spelling
g. ____ writing of history
h. ____ ancient inscriptions
i. ____ very low temperatures
j. ____ human populations

Section Eight

Medical Specialties

71. adenology

72. exodontist

73. proctology
74. osteopathy
75. internist
76. roentgenology

77. orthodontics
78. nephrology

79. physiatrist
80. neonatology

a. ____ use of x rays for diagnosis and treatment of diseases
b. ____ treats disorders of the rectum and anus
c. ____ treats kidneys
d. ____ treats malformed teeth
e. ____ treats newborn
f. ____ uses physical therapy for treatment and rehabilitation
g. ____ study of glands
h. ____ diagnosis and nonsurgical treatment of disease
i. ____ extraction of teeth
j. ____ emphasizes manipulation of the skeleton to treat illnesses.

Section Nine

Fear of ...

81. autophobia
82. zoophobia
83. ailurophobia
84. xenophobia
85. cyanophobia
86. pyrophobia
87. triskaidekaphobia
88. agoraphobia
89. acrophobia
90. necrophobia

a. ____ the number 13
b. ____ dogs
c. ____ open spaces
d. ____ death
e. ____ aloneness
f. ____ heights
g. ____ animals
h. ____ strangers
i. ____ fire
j. ____ cats

7 ©

Section Ten

Measurement

91. chorometry   a. ____ measurement of temperatures greater than 1500 degrees Celsius

92. telemetry   b. ____ accurate measurement of very short intervals of time

93. stereometry   c. ____ measuring and analyzing gasses

94. chronoscopy   d. ____ measuring the size of the universe

95. pyrometry   e. ____ long distance measurement

96. cryometry   f. ____ measuring bones

97. eudiometry   g. ____ determining volume and dimensions of a solid

98. osteometry   h. ____ science of measurement

99. cosmometry   i. ____ land surveying

100. mensuration   j. ____ measurement of extreme low temperatures

Section Eleven

Instruments

101. dosimeter   a. ____ measures revolutions per minute

102. manometer   b. ____ counts revolutions of a wheel

103. odometer   c. ____ measures vertical and horizontal angles

104. tachometer   d. ____ marks time in music

105. altimeter   e. ____ records elapsed distances

106. theodolite   f. ____ measures amount of moisture in the air

107. hydrometer   g. ____ measures pressure of gasses

108. metronome   h. ____ measures specific gravity of liquids

109. cyclometer   i. ____ determines altitude using difference in air pressure

110. hygrometer   j. ____ worn to measure amount of radiation exposure

We are wide-eyed in contemplating the possibility that life may exist elsewhere in the universe, but we wear blinders when contemplating the possibilities of life on earth.
—Norman Cousins

8 ©

Section Twelve   Instruments

111. seismograph   a. ____ extremely accurate timing device
112. tachymeter   b. ____ measures wavelengths and extremely small distances
113. pedometer   c. ____ measures distances travelled on foot
114. barometer   d. ____ measures flatness of a machined surface
115. chronometer   e. ____ measures intensity of earth tremors
116. sextant   f. ____ records movements of the chest during respiration
117. interferometer   g. ____ measures atmospheric pressure
118. planimeter   h. ____ surveying instrument to measure distance, height, etc.
119. galvanometer   i. ____ used to determine latitude and longitude
120. pneumatograph   j. ____ measures the strength and direction of an electric current

Section Thirteen   Isms

121. absolutism   a. ____ repeated criminal behavior
122. conservatism   b. ____ dislike, distrust of all people
123. anthropomorphism   c. ____ excessively optimistic outlook
124. paternalism   d. ____ to retain what is established
125. utopianism   e. ____ prolonged ill health
126. misanthropism   f. ____ parent-like control over subordinates
127. factionism   g. ____ views of a visionary
128. Micawberism   h. ____ complete and unrestricted power of the government
129. recidivism   i. ____ a clique within a larger organization
130. invalidism   j. ____ assigning human attributes to animals, gods

An optimist may see a light where there is none, but why must the
pessimist always run to blow it out?
—Michel De Saint-Pierre

9 ©

Section Fourteen   Isms

131. protectionism	a. ____	derivation of names from person, places, etc.
132. fascism	b. ____	expressing self-exaltation
133. eponymism	c. ____	belief in only one god
134. cronyism	d. ____	extreme national loyalty that is hostile to other nations
135. egalitarianism	e. ____	someone acting abnormally childlike
136. infantilism	f. ____	false argument to deceive someone
137. egotism	g. ____	favoritism
138. sophism	h. ____	developing industry through high tariffs
139. jingoism	i. ____	asserts equality of all people
140. monotheism	j. ____	centralized, nationalistic, totalitarian government

I know that God will not give me anything I can't handle,
I just wish that He didn't trust me so much.
—St. Teresa

One can never consent to creep
when one feels an impulse to soar.
—Helen Keller

When you find yourself in a hole,
the best thing you can do is stop digging.
—Warren Buffet

Put all your eggs in one basket and
— WATCH THAT BASKET.
—Mark Twain

Courage is the price that life extracts
for granting peace.
—Amelia Earhart

Foreign Words and Phrases

Fill in the blank with the number of the matching word(s).

Section One

1. a cappella
2. carte blanche
3. chutzpa
4. machismo
5. vis-à-vis
6. rapprochement
7. sans
8. bon mot
9. milieu
10. alter ego

a. _____ witty saying
b. _____ face to face
c. _____ one's other self
d. _____ unaccompanied choral music
e. _____ unmitigated effrontery
f. _____ environment
g. _____ unlimited authority
h. _____ establishment of cordial relations
i. _____ masculine pride
j. _____ without

Section Two

11. a la carte
12. fait accompli
13. maître d'hôtel
14. tour de force
15. sine qua non
16. bourgeois
17. c'est la vie
18. de rigueur
19. en route
20. in extremis

a. _____ feat of skill
b. _____ that's life
c. _____ near death
d. _____ accomplished fact
e. _____ required by current fashion, custom
f. _____ according to the menu
g. _____ along the way
h. _____ middle-class
i. _____ headwaiter
j. _____ essential

Section Three

21. perestroika
22. abattoir
23. cul-de-sac
24. glasnost
25. mea culpa
26. parvenu
27. lebensraum
28. avant-garde
29. paramour
30. roué

a. _____ immoral man
b. _____ my fault
c. _____ new movement leaders
d. _____ illicit sexual partner
e. _____ living space
f. _____ openness, freedom
g. _____ slaughterhouse
h. _____ blind alley
i. _____ restructuring
j. _____ newly rich

Even if you're on the right track,
you'll get run over if you just sit there.   —Will Rogers

Section Four

31.	détente	a. _____	school attended
32.	ad infinitum	b. _____	altogether
33.	bona fide	c. _____	relaxing, easing
34.	double entendre	d. _____	at first sight
35.	esprit de corps	e. _____	authentic, genuine
36.	in toto	f. _____	a summary
37.	magnum opus	g. _____	double meaning, two interpretations
38.	prima facie	h. _____	without end
39.	résumé	i. _____	single great work
40.	alma mater	j. _____	enthusiasm within a group

Section Five

41.	gestalt	a. _____	spontaneously
42.	in vivo	b. _____	spirit of the times
43.	pro forma	c. _____	per person
44.	sotto voce	d. _____	live
45.	zeitgeist	e. _____	prior to the Civil War
46.	leitmotif	f. _____	unified pattern
47.	ad lib	g. _____	very softly, in an undertone
48.	ante bellum	h. _____	amount
49.	per capita	i. _____	dominant recurring theme
50.	quantum	j. _____	as a matter of form, a gesture

Section Six

51.	scenario	a. _____	blame
52.	in situ	b. _____	normal position
53.	errata	c. _____	an outline of events that may occur
54.	apropos	d. _____	insinuation
55.	per diem	e. _____	errors in written matter
56.	situs	f. _____	social error
57.	ex parte	g. _____	in its original place
58.	innuendo	h. _____	relevant, incidentally
59.	faux pas	i. _____	on one side only
60.	onus	j. _____	per day allowance

I cannot give you the formula for success, but I can give you the
formula for failure — which is: Try to please everybody.
—Herbert B. Swope

Section Seven

61. non sequitur	a. _____	in proportion
62. art nouveau	b. _____	the highest degree
63. chargé d'affaires	c. _____	according to value
64. coup d'etat	d. _____	in disguise
65. summa cum laude	e. _____	new art style
66. incognito	f. _____	violent overthrow of a government
67. ne plus ultra	g. _____	lower rank diplomat
68. R.S.V.P.	h. _____	with highest honors
69. pro rata	i. _____	does not follow logically
70. ad valorem	j. _____	please reply

Section Eight

71. scintilla	a. _____	high fashion
72. quasi	b. _____	by the law itself
73. juggernaut	c. _____	in this year
74. sub rosa	d. _____	very small amount
75. raison d'être	e. _____	afternoon performance
76. hoc anno	f. _____	almost
77. matinée	g. _____	the reason something exists
78. haute couture	h. _____	acceptable person
79. persona grata	i. _____	in secret
80. ipso jure	j. _____	massive force

Section Nine

81. amicus curiae	a. _____	enthusiasm
82. a priori	b. _____	fate
83. potpourri	c. _____	in reality
84. ergo	d. _____	having social skills
85. savoir faire	e. _____	friend of the court
86. en masse	f. _____	bad faith
87. de facto	g. _____	therefore
88. brio	h. _____	from cause to effect
89. mala fide	i. _____	as a whole
90. kismet	j. _____	miscellaneous collection

If we open a quarrel between the past and the present, we shall find
that we have lost the future.
—Winston Churchill

13 ©

Section Ten

91. status quo	a. _____	public opinion
92. ennui	b. _____	unsophistication
93. naïveté	c. _____	intended for the public good
94. cavalier	d. _____	the way things are
95. caveat	e. _____	official persecution of a specific minority
96. déjà vu	f. _____	a knight
97. vox populi	g. _____	illusion of having experienced something before
98. modus operandi	h. _____	caution, warning
99. pogrom	i. _____	method of doing something
100. pro bono public	j. _____	boredom

Section Eleven

101. quid pro quo	a. _____	seize the day, make the most of today
102. ars gratia artis	b. _____	from many, one
103. corpus delicti	c. _____	standing in place of a parent
104. homo sapiens	d. _____	by one's self
105. in loco parentis	e. _____	not of sound mind
106. carpe diem	f. _____	human being
107. non compos mentis	g. _____	evidence to prove a crime occurred
108. per se	h. _____	art for art's sake
109. e pluribus unum	i. _____	very learned person, genius
110. savant	j. _____	one thing in exchange for another

Section Twelve

111. sauté	a. _____	meeting of persons attempting to communicate with the dead
112. dilettante	b. _____	a yellowish brown color
113. buffet	c. _____	to fry lightly in fat
114. ménage	d. _____	a long arduous journey
115. séance	e. _____	social status or position
116. ad hoc	f. _____	person who dabbles in a field of interest
117. khaki	g. _____	a finishing blow or stroke
118. trek	h. _____	meal at which guests serve themselves
119. coup de grâce	i. _____	for a specific situation
120. caste	j. _____	a household

You must have chaos within you to be able to give birth to a dancing star.
—Frederick Nietzche

14 ©

Confusing Words Matching Columns

Fill in the blanks with the number of the matching word. Use a thesaurus and a dictionary to write at least one synonym for each word in the first column. Synonym answers can be found in Answer Key #2.

Section One

1. antecedence	a. ____ exclusive group	1. _____
2. cliche	b. ____ unfairness	_____
3. antecedent	c. ____ priority	_____
4. examine	d. ____ to intrude	_____
5. impinge	e. ____ predecessor	_____
6. inequity	f. ____ infamy	_____
7. inspect	g. ____ trite phrase	_____
8. infringe	h. ____ to determine condition	_____
9. iniquity	i. ____ search for flaws	_____
10. clique	j. ____ intrude	_____

Section Two

11. meet	a. ____ coiled, circular appearance	11. _____
12. requirement	b. ____ rapid, circular motion	_____
13. ardor	c. ____ overtake in the same direction	_____
14. whirl	d. ____ something wanted	_____
15. passion	e. ____ indispensable	_____
16. pass	f. ____ come from opposite directions	_____
17. glance	g. ____ brief incomplete view	_____
18. whorl	h. ____ short-lived strong feeling	_____
19. glimpse	i. ____ overpowering feeling	_____
20. requisite	j. ____ brief quick look	_____

Section Three

21. amount	a. ____ in addition to	21. _____
22. beside	b. ____ pertaining to war	_____
23. persecute	c. ____ protect against loss	_____
24. marital	d. ____ legal procedure	_____
25. ensure	e. ____ pertaining to marriage	_____
26. quantity	f. ____ at the side of	_____
27. prosecute	g. ____ make certain	_____
28. martial	h. ____ something measured	_____
29. insure	i. ____ to oppress	_____
30. besides	j. ____ bulk	_____

Section Four

31. accept	a. ____ any single person	31. _____
32. anyone	b. ____ comparison	_____
33. implicit	c. ____ easily understood	_____
34. except	d. ____ something that completes	_____
35. then	e. ____ flattering remark	_____
36. complement	f. ____ hinted	_____
37. than	g. ____ at that time	_____
38. compliment	h. ____ anybody	_____
39. explicit	i. ____ to exclude	_____
40. any one	j. ____ to receive	_____

Section Five

41. bring	a. ____ to place	41. _____
42. can	b. ____ permit	_____
43. emigrate	c. ____ go forward	_____
44. take	d. ____ to enter a country	_____
45. precede	e. ____ has the ability to do	_____
46. set	f. ____ to be seated	_____
47. immigrate	g. ____ move something away	_____
48. proceed	h. ____ to leave the country	_____
49. sit	i. ____ move toward you	_____
50. may	j. ____ come before	_____

Section Six

51. principal	a. ____ naive	51. _____
52. lie	b. ____ to place	_____
53. ingenious	c. ____ general amount	_____
54. principle	d. ____ unlawful	_____
55. fewer	e. ____ bring out	_____
56. elicit	f. ____ to recline	_____
57. ingenuous	g. ____ sum of money	_____
58. less	h. ____ basic truth	_____
59. illicit	i. ____ counted items	_____
60. lay	j. ____ clever	_____

The best thing about the future is that it comes one day at a time.
—Abraham Lincoln

Section Seven

61.	farther	a. ____	unfavorable	61.	_____
62.	continual	b. ____	opposed		_____
63.	capital	c. ____	misconception		
64.	allusion	d. ____	building		
65.	further	e. ____	extended without interruption		_____
66.	averse	f. ____	a city		_____
67.	capitol	g. ____	quantity, degree		_____
68.	continuous	h. ____	distances		_____
69.	illusion	i. ____	indirect reference		_____
70.	adverse	j. ____	repeated regularly		_____

Section Eight

71.	resumé	a. ____	measures vision	71.	_____
72.	suit	b. ____	things constituting a series		_____
73.	optician	c. ____	to begin anew		_____
74.	lessee	d. ____	to plan		_____
75.	resume	e. ____	give a lease		_____
76.	device	f. ____	a set		_____
77.	suite	g. ____	makes eyeglasses		_____
78.	lessor	h. ____	summary		_____
79.	devise	i. ____	tenant		_____
80.	optometrist	j. ____	mechanical appliance		_____

Once there was a flock of geese. They were kept in a wire cage by a farmer. One day, one of the geese looked up and saw that there was no top to the cage. Excitedly, he told the other geese:
"Look, look! There is no top. We may leave here. We may become free."
Few listened, and none would turn his head to the sky. So, one day he simply spread his wings and flew away — alone.
—Soren Kerkegaard

People are always blaming their circumstances for what they are.
I don't believe in circumstances.
The people who get on in this world are the people
who get up and look for the circumstances they want,
and, if they can't find them, make them.
—George Bernard Shaw

Similar Word Columns

Fill in the blanks with the number of the matching word.

Section One

1. deprecate
2. depreciate
3. fortuitous
4. gratuitous
5. amend
6. emend
7. inchoate
8. chaotic
9. discomforted
10. discomfited
11. venal
12. venial
13. militate
14. mitigate
15. capricious
16. captious
17. definite
18. definitive
19. esoteric
20. exotic

a. ____ hinder
b. ____ happening by chance
c. ____ abstruse, difficult to understand
d. ____ frustrated
e. ____ foreign
f. ____ specific
g. ____ reject
h. ____ apt to change suddenly
i. ____ alter by adding
j. ____ corrupt
k. ____ make milder
l. ____ unwarranted
m. ____ take out errors
n. ____ eager to catch others in a mistake
o. ____ rudimentary, not fully formed
p. ____ conclusive
q. ____ belittle
r. ____ embarrassed
s. ____ excusable, pardonable
t. ____ confused

Section Two

21. turbid
22. turgid
23. censor
24. censure
25. equable
26. equitable
27. precipitate
28. precipitous
29. complacent
30. complaisant
31. judicial
32. judicious
33. prescribe
34. proscribe
35. chary
36. wary
37. official
38. officious
39. deduce
40. deduct

a. ____ steady, uniform
b. ____ disinterested, fair
c. ____ self-satisfied
d. ____ to conclude from evidence
e. ____ suspicious
f. ____ muddy, cloudy
g. ____ authoritative standing
h. ____ hasty, rash
i. ____ prohibit, forbid
j. ____ reprimand, rebuke
k. ____ carefulness, discretion
l. ____ subtract
m. ____ just, fair
n. ____ obliging, affable
o. ____ wise, prudent
p. ____ swollen, pompous
q. ____ meddlesome, interfering
r. ____ steep, abrupt
s. ____ lay down rules, to order
t. ____ suppress, delete

18 ©

Eponym Matching Columns

Fill in the blanks with the number of the matching word(s).

Section One

1. Hobson's choice	a. ____	fanatically committed to a cause
2. Faustian	b. ____	impossible or foolish fancy
3. Byzantine	c. ____	imminent danger
4. chimera	d. ____	lack of an alternative
5. meander	e. ____	ambiguous
6. galvanize	f. ____	bureaucratic complexity
7. Delphic	g. ____	indicates relative hardness of minerals and stones
8. zealot	h. ____	to arouse into awareness
9. Sword of Damocles	i. ____	worldly, devilish
10. Mohs' scale	j. ____	follow a winding route

Section Two

11. aegis	a. ____	intellectual relationship, friendship
12. Baedeker	b. ____	economic theories
13. taciturn	c. ____	protection, patronage
14. stygian	d. ____	nightmarish, surreal
15. platonic	e. ____	not talkative
16. Kafkaesque	f. ____	crafty, deceitful, cunning
17. Gresham's law	g. ____	a guidebook
18. draconian	h. ____	dark, gloomy
19. Machiavellian	i. ____	bad money will drive good money out of circulation
20. Keynesian	j. ____	harsh, cruel

Section Three

21. Wassermann test	a. ____	actor or actress
22. vulcanize	b. ____	accidently making a fortuitous discovery
23. Schick test	c. ____	diagnostic test for syphilis
24. utopia	d. ____	vaccine preventing polio
25. Spartan	e. ____	process to increase the strength of rubber
26. serendipity	f. ____	to be obdurate, refuse to answer
27. Salk vaccine	g. ____	idealized place, political perfection
28. stoical	h. ____	warlike, stoical, severe
29. stonewall	i. ____	test to determine immunity to diphtheria
30. thespian	j. ____	enduring, brave

19 ©

Section Four

31. Xanadu	a. ____ long distance race
32. Stradavarius	b. ____ unit of electric current
33. eponym	c. ____ chorea, involuntary jerking movements
34. ampere	d. ____ unit of magnetism
35. Charcot's Disease	e. ____ valuable violin
36. Hansen's Disease	f. ____ place of idyllic beauty
37. marathon	g. ____ unit of electrical resistance
38. Saint Vitus' Dance	h. ____ leprosy
39. ohm	i. ____ multiple sclerosis
40. gauss	j. ____ real or mythological persons or places which are the source of a name of an era, event, or object

God gave me the stubbornness of a mule
and a fairly keen scent.
—Albert Einstein

Most of us go through life not knowing we want,
but feeling darned sure this isn't it.
—Anonymous

Never go to a doctor whose office plants have died.
—Erma Bombeck

My barn having burned to the ground,
I can now see the moon.
—Japanese maxim

Fall seven times, stand up eight.
—Japanese proverb

When life throws you a curve, it's to teach you how to bend.
—Anonymous

If you want a place in the sun,
you must leave the shade of the family tree.
—Osage proverb

Eponym Word Definitions

Select the correct word(s) that most nearly defines the following statements.

1. A theory which maintains that increasing tax rates causes a reduction in revenues:
    a. Laffer Curve   ____
    b. Ginnie Mae
    c. Keynesian
    d. arbitrage

2. Very small, tiny:
    a. gargantuan   ____
    b. Lilith
    c. Lilliputian
    d. febrile

3. A five-line nonsense rhyme:
    a. sonnet   ____
    b. limerick
    c. drivel
    d. prattle

4. A progressive, irreversible degenerative disease of the brain cells:
    a. Kaposi's Carcinoma   ____
    b. Hodgkin's Disease
    c. Alzheimer's Disease
    d. Charcot's Syndrome

5. Sluggish, morose, taciturn:
    a. genial   ____
    b. garrulous
    c. loquacious
    d. saturnine

6. A method of natural childbirth:
    a. Lamarkian   ____
    b. Lamaze
    c. Neronian
    d. Peter Principle

7. A seducer of women:
    a. Galahad   ____
    b. Coulomb
    c. Svengali
    d. Don Juan

21 ©

8. The ratio of the speed of an object to the speed of sound:
    a. Mach number
    b. Avogadro's number
    c. Boyle's law
    d. Binet Scale

    _____

9. Heavy fortifications built by the French before World War II:
    a. Ypres Salient
    b. Siegfried Line
    c. Maginot Line
    d. Normandy Line

    _____

10. Ludicrous misuse of words:
    a. neologism
    b. malapropism
    c. spoonerism
    d. sobriquet

    _____

11. A strict disciplinarian, stickler for rigid rules:
    a. Hegelian
    b. martinet
    c. stoic
    d. penologist

    _____

12. Foolishly and tearfully sentimental:
    a. maudlin
    b. affected
    c. kitsch
    d. romanticist

    _____

13. A person who takes an independent stand:
    a. tributary
    b. eristic
    c. sovereign
    d. maverick

    _____

14. A wise, loyal adviser:
    a. exhorter
    b. mentor
    c. patron
    d. propagandist

    _____

We can secure other people's approval, if we do right and try hard;
but our own is worth a hundred of it.
—Mark Twain

22 ©

15. Quick-witted, volatile, fickle:
    a. gaseous
    b. compulsive
    c. mercurial
    d. spasmodic

    _____

16. Anyone or anything which might defeat or frustrate someone:
    a. nemesis
    b. confounder
    c. instigator
    d. defaulter

    _____

17. The principle according to which the best explanation of an event is the one that is the simplest:
    a. Pythagorean Theorem
    b. Ptolomey's Theory
    c. Gnosticism
    d. Occam's Razor

    _____

18. Extended, adventurous wandering:
    a. serendipity
    b. odyssey
    c. traversing
    d. perambulating

    _____

19. Principles of hereditary phenomena:
    a. Pascal's laws
    b. Boyle's laws
    c. Mendel's laws
    d. Murphy's law

    _____

20. Self-love, excessive interest in one's appearance:
    a. brashness
    b. narcissism
    c. sadism
    d. masochism

    _____

21. Any bitter verbal attack:
    a. philippic
    b. nuncupative
    c. impassioned
    d. all of the above

    _____

Science is nothing but trained and organized common sense.
—T. H. Huxley, 1894

22. A foolishly optimistic person:
    a. Chaplinesque
    b. auspicious
    c. despondent
    d. Pollyanna   ____

23. A too costly victory:
    a. Neronian
    b. Pyrrhic
    c. Graustarkean
    d. Miltonic   ____

24. Caught up in the romance of noble deeds or unreasonable ideas:
    a. materialistic
    b. cynic
    c. self-indulgent
    d. quixotic   ____

25. A scale by which the magnitudes of earthquakes are measured:
    a. Mohs'
    b. Kelvin
    c. Celsius
    d. Richter   ____

I learned the way a monkey learns —
by watching its parents.
—Queen Elizabeth II

Have no fear of perfection;
you'll never reach it.
—Salvador Dali

I keep my ideals because in spite of everything,
I still believe people are really good at heart.
—Anne Frank

No man really becomes a fool
until he stops asking questions.
—Charles Steinmetz

Weak desires bring weak results,
just as a small amount of fire makes a small amount of heat.
—Napoleon Hill

Word Division Hyphenation

Correct the words having incorrect word division. Use the most accepted rules for syllabication based on pronunciation rather than derivations or roots.

Section One

1. nap-alm _____
2. ra-con-teur _____
3. a-maze _____
4. should-n't _____
5. appli-cable _____
6. ti-til-late _____
7. ra-cial _____
8. dif-fer _____
9. ma-gi-cal _____
10. brac-ing _____

Section Two

11. im-per-ative _____
12. ub-iety _____
13. sel-lers _____
14. co-in-cide _____
15. rhy-thm _____
16. bra-cer _____

17. sur-geon _____
18. inter-rogate _____
19. over-active _____
20. naph-tha _____

Section Three

21. child-ren _____
22. re-ferral _____
23. par-al-ysis _____
24. sta-sis _____
25. co-dicil _____
26. per-imeter _____
27. mac-ad-am _____
28. ga-laxy _____
29. min-ia-ture _____
30. ma-chine-gun _____

Section Four

31. feu-dal _____
32. in-ter-roga-tive _____
33. va-li-dity _____
34. sta-tis-ti-cal _____
35. vali-da-tion _____
36. in-to _____
37. forma-tive _____
38. intro-spec-tion _____
39. un-do _____
40. sta-tis-ti-cian _____

Section Five

41. form-al-ize _____
42. a-nec-do-tal _____
43. the-ra-pist _____
44. zo-olo-gist _____
45. urolo-gist _____
46. fid-get _____

47. mi-crobe _____
48. vacu-um _____
49. bi-sym-me-try _____
50. a-men-able _____

Section Six

51. var-ied _____
52. bi-stro _____
53. xe-non _____
54. wake-ful-ness _____
55. a-nal-ogy _____
56. vari-et-al _____
57. cate-gor-ical _____
58. you're _____
59. icono-clast _____
60. un-ani-mous _____

Anytime you don't want a thing, you get it. —Calvin Coolidge

25 ©

Section Seven

61. co-ef-fi-cient   _____
62. the-o-logi-cal   _____
63. het-ero-doxy   _____
64. par-al-lel   _____
65. refer-ed   _____
66. pa-ral-lyse   _____
67. the-at-ri-cal   _____
68. fe-ud   _____
69. mac-aw   _____
70. peri-stal-sis   _____

Section Eight

71. anemic   _____
72. psy-cho-gen-esis _____
73. bi-on-ic   _____
74. ca-rou-sel   _____
75. ur-ol-ogy   _____
76. exon-er-a-tion   _____
77. hel-lish   _____
78. sy-ba-rite   _____
79. dep-u-tize   _____
80. bio-sphere   _____

Section Nine

81. psy-cholo-gist   _____
82. kind-red-ship   _____
83. hel-lo   _____
84. fi-bula   _____
85. gen-e-al-o-gist   _____
86. zo-o-logi-cal   _____
87. ca-ro-tid   _____
88. des-pon-dent   _____
89. kin-dling   _____
90. ex-odus   _____

Section Ten

91.   kinder-gar-ten   _____
92.   mal-aise   _____
93.   ne-glect-ful   _____
94.   pa-rox-ysm   _____
95.   fruit-ion   _____
96.   Xe-rox   _____
97.   jumpi-ly   _____
98.   li-ga-ture   _____
99.   opu-lent   _____
100. qual-ity   _____

Section Eleven

101. icon-og-raphy   _____
102. par-ol   _____
103. lia-ble   _____
104. un-an-nounced   _____
105. knowl-edge   _____
106. na-tur-al-is-tic   _____
107. qual-ify   _____
108. seri-al-ly   _____
109. jumpoff   _____
110. medi-cal   _____

Section Twelve

111. man-ag-er   _____
112. tin-gly   _____
113. ra-dio-gra-phic   _____
114. o-bli-ging   _____
115. ma-na-ger-i-al   _____
116. to-pic   _____
117. ra-di-ol-o-gist   _____
118. ne-gli-gent   _____
119. i-so-mer   _____
120. medi-ci-nal   _____

Rule #1: "Don't sweat the small stuff."
Rule #2: "Everything is small stuff."
        —Van Halen

Nothing exists except atoms and empty space; everything else is opinion. —Democritus

26 ©

CHAPTER 2: WORD MECHANICS

Misspelled Words

Correct the misspelled word in each group in the first space provided. Write a **synonym and antonym** for the word which has an asterisk after it in the second space provided.

1. a. genteel * _____
    b. herniated
    c. accomotate _____
    d. adolescent

2. a. ingeneous _____
    b. abettor *
    c. aneurysm _____
    d. trafficking

3. a. affidavit _____
    b. fluorscent
    c. laborious * _____
    d. malleable

4. a. millenium _____
    b. in absentia
    c. incorrigible * _____
    d. erythrocyte

5. a. hypothetical * _____
    b. laryngitis
    c. evidentiary _____
    d. cognative

6. a. demagogue * _____
    b. hemorrhage
    c. deponent _____
    d. abcess

7. a. embarassment _____
    b. enervate
    c. assimilate * _____
    d. tantamount

8. a. writing _____
    b. confetti
    c. handicaped _____
    d. written *

9. a. nickle _____
    b. certiorari
    c. mammogram _____
    d. chauvinist *

10. a. escheat _____
    b. tourniquet
    c. fiat * _____
    d. optholmologist

11. a. execution _____
    b. endocrine
    c. appelant _____
    d. petulant *

12. a. legible _____
    b. renumeration
    c. herniated _____
    d. redundant *

13. a. cemetary _____
    b. impervious *
    c. malignancy _____
    d. exacerbation

14. a. conciliatory _____
    b. personell
    c. inertia _____
    d. achievement *

15. a. anachronism _____
    b. preceeding
    c. fraudulent * _____
    d. debility

16. a. exteriorize _____
    b. thromboid
    c. mortgagable _____
    d. emollient *

27 ©

17.   a. coronor
      b. anorexia
      c. congressionally
      d. gruesome *

18.   a. saboteur
      b. amniocentesis
      c. impecunious *
      d. mollases

19.   a. occuring
      b. miscegenation
      c. perfidious *
      d. occur

20.   a. studying
      b. euphimism
      c. totaled
      d. efface *

21.   a. casuistry *
      b. purveyor
      c. metastasis
      d. minutescule

22.   a. coalesce *
      b. thoracic
      c. prognosticate
      d. unconsionability

23.   a. cranium
      b. malediction *
      c. excission
      d. deductibility

24.   a. trenchent *
      b. malevolent
      c. commingle
      d. pusillanimous

25.   a. demur *
      b. repertoir
      c. cartilage
      d. paradigm

26.   a. perspicacious *
      b. colostomy
      c. herbevorous
      d. quintuplicate

27.   a. Massachusets
      b. semiautonomous
      c. rancor *
      d. perspicacity

28.   a. corporeal
      b. ignominy *
      c. matrilineage
      d. disinfranchise

29.   a. incedently
      b. apposite
      c. phlegmatic *
      d. panegyric

30.   a. loquascious *
      b. impracticability
      c. raucous
      d. leukemia

31.   a. parliament
      b. breadth *
      c. poliomylitis
      d. attainder

32.   a. transference
      b. restaraunt
      c. subsidiary *
      d. staphylococcus

33.   a. irrelevant *
      b. diarrhea
      c. violance
      d. artifice

34.   a. extrordinary *
      b. misfeasance
      c. osteoporoses
      d. receive

35.   a. characteristic *
      b. esophagus
      c. quiescent
      d. priviledge

36.   a. hepatitis
      b. believe *
      c. chocalate
      d. nunc pro tunc

28 ©

37. a. ameliorate *   _____
     b. larynx
     c. nefarious   _____
     d. patercidal

38. a. complascent   _____
     b. caveat *
     c. cataclysm   _____
     d. etiology

39. a. rapprochment   _____
     b. subpoena
     c. incommunicado   _____
     d. noisome *

40. a. frolick   _____
     b. Connecticut
     c. commitment *   _____
     d. emphysema

41. a. Louisiana   _____
     b. corruptability
     c. intermittent   _____
     d. commit *

42. a. dossier   _____
     b. pharmaceutical
     c. accesible   _____
     d. altruistic *

43. a. liason *   _____
     b. aneurysm
     c. mendicant   _____
     d. preliminary

44. a. paroxysm   _____
     b. egress *
     c. supersede   _____
     d. extrapate

45. a. surcease *   _____
     b. excruciating
     c. predetory   _____
     d. rationale

46. a. sebaceous   _____
     b. archetype *
     c. airosol   _____
     d. procuring

47. a. temperature   _____
     b. advacate
     c. tragedy *   _____
     d. flaccid

48. a. stoping   _____
     b. hindrance
     c. perennial *   _____
     d. stratagem

49. a. prohibitery *   _____
     b. tertiary
     c. parthenogenesis   _____
     d. benefiting

50. a. evanescent *   _____
     b. connivance
     c. dispondent   _____
     d. ambivalence

51. a. raucous   _____
     b. aciduous
     c. munificently *   _____
     d. hereditament

52. a. compliant *   _____
     b. vociferous
     c. inheritance   _____
     d. consulltant

53. a. ostracize   _____
     b. complaint *
     c. fuseladge   _____
     d. hemiplegia

54. a. soveriegn   _____
     b. syndrome
     c. vendor *   _____
     d. prima facie

55. a. subornation   _____
     b. foreigner *
     c. subsistance   _____
     d. eczema

56. a. prodigal   _____
     b. pacifism *
     c. aurora borealis   _____
     d. sacreligious

57. a. superannuation   _____
     b. halcyon
     c. termagant *   _____
     d. berift

58. a. laborynth   _____
     b. vitiate
     c. monopolize *   _____
     d. susceptible

59. a. recumbent *   _____
     b. defendant
     c. pervaricate   _____
     d. bailsmen

60. a. effrontery *   _____
     b. prophylaxis
     c. abstemious   _____
     d. decedant

61. a. surebuttal   _____
     b. arrythmia
     c. juridical   _____
     d. penchant *

62. a. escheet   _____
     b. actinic
     c. filch *   _____
     d. machinations

63. a. cognizant *   _____
     b. nonfeasance
     c. pseudonim   _____
     d. savant

64. a. weal   _____
     b. incompatible *
     c. litigous   _____
     d. paean

65. a. assuage *   _____
     b. aggrandise
     c. escarpment   _____
     d. indicia

66. a. opprobrium   _____
     b. tonsillectomy
     c. condign *   _____
     d. corpulant

67. a. mulct   _____
     b. oscilate *
     c. resourceful   _____
     d. administratrix

68. a. chiropractor   _____
     b. cursory *
     c. geneology   _____
     d. sepulcher

69. a. stopgap   _____
     b. ostracise
     c. oblique *   _____
     d. stoppage

70. a. hageography   _____
     b. omnivorous
     c. demure *   _____
     d. phlebitis

71. a. urbane *   _____
     b. pastiche
     c. aplombe   _____
     d. fidgety

72. a. pogrom   _____
     b. prevalent *
     c. sciatica   _____
     d. antetheses

73. a. gauche *   _____
     b. menagery
     c. hypoglycemia   _____
     d. schism

74. a. kibitz   _____
     b. fiasco *
     c. fulminating   _____
     d. cognoman

75. a. potpourri   _____
     b. mountebank
     c. inexorable *   _____
     d. exogenious

76. a. chary   _____
     b. vappid *
     c. voyeur   _____
     d. anesthesiologist

30 ©

77. a. emoluement   _____   82. a. forethought   _____
    b. ambulatory   b. jeopardy
    c. inchoate *   _____   c. saturnine *   _____
    d. bouquet   d. proseletise

78. a. iatrogenic   _____   83. a. obdurate *   _____
    b. dissonant *   b. hypochondria
    c. torsion   _____   c. chicanary   _____
    d. perpetrater   d. ennui

79. a. macaber   _____   84. a. acquiecence *   _____
    b. concupiscence   b. placebo
    c. adroit *   _____   c. virile   _____
    d. fiduciary   d. palisade

80. a. mediocre *   _____   85. a. preternatural   _____
    b. dyspeptic   b. opullent *
    c. arroyo   _____   c. testosterone   _____
    d. archepelago   d. plenary

81. a. ignominious *   _____   86. a. heinous *   _____

    b. contravene   b. tranquilizer
    c. obiesance   _____   c. percursor   _____
    d. pulchritude   d. exigency

What we see depends mainly on what we look for.
—John Lubbock

To be wronged is nothing unless you continue to remember it.
— Confucius

The stars receive their brightness from the surrounding dark.
—Dante

Reflect on your present blessings,
of which every man has many,
not on your past misfortunes,
of which all men have some.
—Charles Dickens

I stopped believing in Santa Claus
when my mother too me to see him in a department store,
and he asked for my autograph.
—Shirley Temple

31 ©

Misspelled Word Columns

Indicate the correctly spelled word in the space provided. Use a dictionary and a thesaurus to learn the definition, synonyms, and antonyms for any word with which you are unfamiliar.

1.	a. saphire	b. sapphire	_____
2.	a. barbaric	b. barabaric	_____
3.	a. judgeship	b. judgship	_____
4.	a. pungent	b. pungant	_____
5.	a. indices	b. indicis	_____
6.	a. epistlemological	b. epistemological	_____
7.	a. spurious	b. spourious	_____
8.	a. eatrogenic	b. iatrogenic	_____
9.	a. paradime	b. paradigm	_____
10.	a. gnome	b. gnom	_____
11.	a. eminent	b. eminant	_____
12.	a. paralellogram	b. parallelogram	_____
13.	a. subsumed	b. subsummed	_____
14.	a. concommitent	b. concomitant	_____
15.	a. incipiant	b. incipient	_____
16.	a. chanticleer	b. chanticlere	_____
17.	a. hirsute	b. hirsuit	_____
18.	a. nadire	b. nadir	_____
19.	a. centrifugally	b. centrifigurally	_____
20.	a. centerpetally	b. centripetally	_____
21.	a. nebullus	b. nebulas	_____
22.	a. anomaly	b. anamoly	_____
23.	a. exterpolation	b. extrapolation	_____
24.	a. debauch	b. debauche	_____
25.	a. solon	b. sollon	_____
26.	a. cadraes	b. cadres	_____
27.	a. regaled	b. regalled	_____
28.	a. pettyfogery	b. pettifoggery	_____
29.	a. matric	b. matrix	_____
30.	a. plutocracy	b. plutokracy	_____
31.	a. vignettes	b. vignets	_____
32.	a. eschewed	b. eschewd	_____
33.	a. fattuity	b. fatuity	_____
34.	a. alchemy	b. alchemistry	_____
35.	a. protogonists	b. protagonists	_____
36.	a. ersatz	b. ersats	_____
37.	a. kaleidoscope	b. keiladascope	_____
38.	a. leviethons	b. leviathans	_____
39.	a. business	b. bussness	_____
40.	a. relevent	b. relevant	_____

41. a. mischievous   b. mischievious   ____
42. a. kichken   b. kitchen   ____
43. a. insouceant   b. insouciant   ____
44. a. idiosyncratic   b. ideosyncratic   ____
45. a. henceforth   b. hencforth   ____
46. a. gaurantee   b. guarantee   ____
47. a. felony   b. fellony   ____
48. a. evulotionary   b. evolutionary   ____
49. a. dramatically   b. dramaticaly   ____
50. a. corderoy   b. corduroy   ____

51. a. boundry   b. boundary   ____
52. a. aristocracy   b. arestocrasy   ____
53. a. indignant   b. indignent   ____
54. a. misfeesance   b. misfeasance   ____
55. a. seismology   b. siesmology   ____
56. a. quintessence   b. quintescence   ____
57. a. profoundity   b. profundity   ____
58. a. omelet   b. omlette   ____
59. a. naivete   b. niavete   ____
60. a. traceable   b. tracible   ____

61. a. siezure   b. seizure   ____
62. a. useable   b. usable   ____
63. a. diplomacy   b. diplomasy   ____
64. a. apostasy   b. apostacy   ____
65. a. offence   b. offense   ____
66. a. mineralogy   b. minerology   ____
67. a. pronunciation   b. pronounciation   ____
68. a. combatent   b. combatant   ____
69. a. commited   b. committed   ____
70. a. seige   b. siege   ____

71. a. barbarous   b. barbrous   ____
72. a. anglicize   b. anglisize   ____
73. a. analize   b. analyze   ____
74. a. supervise   b. supervize   ____
75. a. innoculate   b. inoculate   ____
76. a. cieling   b. ceiling   ____
77. a. codeine   b. codiene   ____
78. a. deceive   b. decieve   ____
79. a. chandellere   b. chandelier   ____
80. a. artisticaly   b. artistically   ____

81.	a. happily	b. happilly	____
82.	a. truely	b. truly	____
83.	a. ninth	b. nineth	____
84.	a. stupify	b. stupefy	____
85.	a. fortify	b. fortefy	____
86.	a. gassing	b. gasing	____
87.	a. gasseous	b. gaseous	____
88.	a. thinner	b. thiner	____
89.	a. abuttment	b. abutment	____
90.	a. admiting	b. admitting	____
91.	a. inhibited	b. inhibitted	____
92.	a. permitted	b. permited	____
93.	a. prefering	b. preferring	____
94.	a. preferential	b. preferrential	____
95.	a. focuses	b. focusus	____
96.	a. confidence	b. confidance	____
97.	a. maintainence	b. maintenance	____
98.	a. monastery	b. monastary	____
99.	a. dictionary	b. dictionery	____
100.	a. collectables	b. collectibles	____
101.	a. counterfeit	b. counterfiet	____
102.	a. detectible	b. detectable	____
103.	a. compromise	b. compromize	____
104.	a. incomprehensable	b. incomprehensible	____
105.	a. supersede	b. superceed	____
106.	a. concede	b. consede	____
107.	a. jingoeism	b. jingoism	____
108.	a. inevetable	b. inevitable	____
109.	a. inflexible	b. inflexable	____
110.	a. contramand	b. countermand	____
111.	a. contraband	b. controband	____
112.	a. misstaken	b. mistaken	____
113.	a. contravert	b. controvert	____
114.	a. discomfitted	b. discomfited	____
115.	a. arraignment	b. arrainement	____
116.	a. forestry	b. forestery	____
117.	a. harpschord	b. harpsichord	____
118.	a. jazmine	b. jasmine	____
119.	a. narcissism	b. narcisism	____
120.	a. poingnent	b. poignant	____

I can complain because rose bushes have thorns or rejoice because thorn bushes have roses. It's all how you look at it. —J. Kenfield Mosley

Misspelled Compound Words

Select the misspelled compound word in each group and write the correct spelling.

1. a. check-up   ____
    b. check-in
    c. night-light
    d. timetable

2. a. daytime   ____
    b. back-up
    c. paper clip
    d. touch-up

3. a. checkoff   ____
    b. spin-off
    c. lift-off
    d. print-out

4. a. in-between   ____
    b. break-through
    c. right-of-way
    d. line of credit

5. a. time-sharing   ____
    b. turnaround
    c. profit-sharing
    d. runaway

6. a. yo-yo   ____
    b. write-off
    c. bi-yearly
    d. runoff

7. a. mix-up   ____
    b. lineup
    c. breakup
    d. signup

8. a. shutin   ____
    b. sell-off
    c. rollback
    d. standout

9. a. skin diving   ____
    b. skyjacker
    c. fact sheet
    d. time-clock

10. a. editor-in-chief   ____
    b. whistle-blower
    c. two-by-four
    d. wear and tear

11. a. cut and dried   ____
    b. payroll
    c. trade-off
    d. day care

12. a. sick pay   ____
    b. light-year
    c. foul-up
    d. strongarm

13. a. light-footed   ____
    b. black-out
    c. mezzo-soprano
    d. T-shirt

14. a. General-Manager Smith   ____
    b. Vice-Consul Jones
    c. Vice President-elect Truman
    d. Attorney General Reno

15. a. grants-in-aid   ____
    b. line of credit
    c. the also rans
    d. pre-engineered

16. a. eye-witness   ____
    b. eye-opener
    c. life span
    d. preeminent

The secret of success is constancy to purpose.
—Benjamin Disraeli

35 ©

17. a. put-down   _____
     b. turndown
     c. voiceover
     d. hangover

18. a. bailout   _____
     b. fallingout
     c. carryings-on
     d. go-between

19. a. machine readable   _____
     b. pullback
     c. layaway
     d. get-together

20. a. place-name   _____
     b. mock-up
     c. mark-up
     d. walk-in

21. a. right of way   _____
     b. rule of thumb
     c. whodunit
     d. ups and downs

22. a. the look-alike   _____
     b. sharptongued
     c. f-stop
     d. V neck

23. a. one-way-street   _____
     b. 35-miles-an-hour speed
     c. a 10 percent increase
     d. off-the-record statement

24. a. Supreme Court decision   _____
     b. Mexican-American restaurant
     c. part time job
     d. all-day test

25. a. a five-and-ten   _____
     b. skill building
     c. shakedown
     d. speed reading

26. a. sign off   _____
     b. turnoff
     c. time-out
     d. handout

27. a. runaround   _____
     b. throwback
     c. inter-face
     d. tryout

28. a. to air-condition   _____
     b. to downgrade
     c. to down-size
     d. to double-space

29. a. to babysit   _____
     b. to highlight
     c. to field-test
     d. to spot-check

30. a. well-known teacher   _____
     b. bandwagon
     c. air bag
     d. high priced articles

31. a. five-color quilt   _____
     b. ad-hoc committee
     c. high-ranking officer
     d. off-the-record statement

32. a. 5-to-1 ratio   _____
     b. 2:1 ratio
     c. tone-deaf
     d. a four-weeks term

33. a. pre-and postnatal care   _____
     b. prehigh-school years
     c. offbeat
     d. self-addressed envelope

34. a. the not too interesting   _____
       lecture
     b. warmed over ideas
     c. go-go dancers
     d. single-or double-spaced

35. a. quasijudicial   ____
     b. grandson
     c. great-uncle
     d. flight attendant

36. a. A-frame   ____
     b. y axis
     c. S curve
     d. H-bomb

37. a. paper work   ____
     b. bank note
     c. hand gun
     d. tip-off

38. a. kilowatt-hour   ____
     b. kickoff
     c. silicon-dioxide
     d. walkie-talkie

39. a. master plan   ____
     b. sub rosa
     c. photo copy
     d. gun rack

40. a. cabdriver   ____
     b. fourth-grader
     c. anti-Semitic
     d. mid-day

41. a. time-piece   ____
     b. by-product
     c. byline
     d. V-8 engine

42. a. safe-deposit   ____
     b. post-mortem
     c. recross-examination
     d. co-defendant

43. a. cross walk   ____
     b. vice president
     c. autosuggestion
     d. stepchild

44. a. trial and error experiment ___
     b. income tax return
     c. random-access memory
     d. to mastermind

45. a. habit-forming   ____
     b. hand-picked
     c. workman
     d. gunshot

46. a. brokenhearted   ____
     b. per diem
     c. good-hearted
     d. tail light

47. a. north-west   ____
     b. north-southeast
     c. prorate
     d. drugstore

48. a. whip lash   ____
     b. white lie
     c. cash crop
     d. per capita

49. a. bird's-eye view   ____
     b. doubledecker
     c. slow-motion vehicle
     d. seat belt

50. a. selfimportant   ____
     b. armrest
     c. antipoverty
     d. two-door

51. a. selfsame   ____
     b. mid-April
     c. co-captain
     d. cosigner

52. a. courthouse   ____
     b. closecaptioned
     c. nonresponsive
     d. court reporter

53. a. pre-empt   ____   59. a. odds and ends   ____
    b. neo-Nazi   b. cooperative
    c. above-mentioned   c. price-earnings
    d. rub-down   d. double parked

54. a. pre-judge   ____   60. a. air-to-ground missile   ____
    b. midwinter   b. co-counsel
    c. crosswalk   c. counter-clockwise
    d. cross-examine   d. in-court discussion

55. a. thereafter   ____   61. a house-warming   ____
    b. exwife   b. blueprint
    c. right-handed   c. nearsighted
    d. out-of-pocket   d. sight-seeing

56. a. courtmartial   ____   62. a. playback   ____
    b. read-only memory   b. free lance
    c. farsighted   c. bookstore
    d. clear-sighted   d. three piece suit

57. a. broad-minded   ____   63. a. to dry-clean   ____
    b. an above-average grade   b. to proofread
    c. air-bags   c. letter-perfect
    d. job action   d. poorly-built car

58. a. an up-and-coming doctor ____   64. a. plea-bargaining   ____
    b. lackluster attitude   b. quasi corporation
    c. inter and intra-state highways   c. coauthor
    d. layoff   d. owner-manager

Do or do not. There is no try.
—Yoda

It isn't for the moment you are stuck that you need courage,
but for the long uphill climb back to security and faith and security.
—Anne Morrow Lindberg

Use the talents you possess,
for the woods would be very silent if no birds sang
except the best.
—Anonymous

If you are naturally kind you attract
a lot of people you don't like.
—William Feather

38 ©

Misspelled Plural Words

Select and correct the misspelled plural word in each group in the space provided.

1. a. accounts payable   ____
   b. crises
   c. traveler's checks
   d. daughter-in-laws

2. a. shampoos   ____
   b. Eskimoes
   c. stimuli
   d. men employees

3. a. addendums   ____
   b. skies
   c. antennas
   d. mestizos

4. a. coats of arm   ____
   b. oases
   c. armadillos
   d. strata

5. a. chassis   ____
   b. passersby
   c. potatos
   d. halves

6. a. attorneys   ____
   b. forefeet
   c. oxen
   d. colloquys

7. a. drooles   ____
   b. notaries public
   c. loci
   d. zeros

8. a. analyses   ____
   b. woman writers
   c. fade-outs
   d. cups full

9. a. hypotheses   ____
   b. larvae
   c. minutiae
   d. tomatos

10. a. virtuosos   ____
    b. surgeons general
    c. thiefs
    d. heroes

11. a. skis   ____
    b. the Alleghenys
    c. the Carolinas
    d. Januarys

12. a. two Kansas Cities   ____
    b. the Rockies
    c. three Timothys
    d. two Douglases

13. a. sheep   ____
    b. tankfuls
    c. tank fulls
    d. lookers-on

14. a. banjos   ____
    b. vetos
    c. infernos
    d. mementos

15. a. talismen   ____
    b. agendas
    c. media
    d. diagnoses

16. a. km   ____
    b. the Joneses
    c. alumnas
    d. tariffs

17. a. sopranos   ____   26. a. pros and cons   ____
     b. letter of credits   b. threes
     c. provost marshals   c. the Romanos
     d. crepes suzette   d. graffitos

18. a. biases   ____   27. a. bookshelves   ____
     b. commodities   b. which's and there's
     c. ratii   c. twenty-sixes
     d. memos   d. in the 1980's

19. a. helixis   ____   28. a. deejays   ____
     b. errata   b. strawberrys
     c. theses   c. minutiae
     d. bills of fare   d. phyla

20. a. algae   ____   29. a. Messrs. Smith and Jones   ____
     b. taxis   b. dogmas
     c. reduction in forces   c. parenthesis
     d. quartzes   d. sequelae

21. a. stereos   ____   30. a. pp 15-37   ____
     b. has-beens   b. pp 5 ff
     c. senators-elect   c. pp 35
     d. hairdoes   d. ll 5-10

22. a. liabilities   ____   31. a. brethren   ____
     b. taxes   b. know-it-alls
     c. soliloquys   c. proofreaders' marks
     d. aides-de-camp   d. proxys

23. a. delivery of the c.o.d.'s   ____   32. a. ellipses   ____
     b. Ph.Ds   b. menservants
     c. ordering W2s   c. deers
     d. genuses   d. tattoos

24. a. pro and cons   ____   33. a. times-out   ____

     b. allies   b. lookers-on
     c. raspberries   c. come-ons
     d. cameos   d. runners-up

25. a. makers-up   ____
     b. highers-up
     c. run-ins
     d. masters at arms

Do not think of study as work. Think of it as an opportunity to learn.
—Albert Einstein
40 ©

Abbreviations

Fill in the blanks with the number of the matching abbreviation.

Section One

1. A.B.	a. ____		doing business as
2. s.d.	b. ____		thus, so
3. pro tem	c. ____		barrels
4. loc. cit.	d. ____		amplitude modulation
5. ibid.	e. ____		bachelor of arts
6. bbls	f. ____		the same place
7. Hz	g. ____		in the place cited
8. sic	h. ____		temporarily
9. AM	i. ____		cycles per second
10. d.b.a.	j. ____		without a date

Section Two

11. Ph.D.	a. ____		Bureau of Indian Affairs
12. viz.	b. ____		consumer price index
13. pH	c. ____		hundredweight
14. op. cit.	d. ____		bachelor of laws
15. BIA	e. ____		doctor of philosophy
16. LL.B.	f. ____		unknown quantity
17. A.M.	g. ____		acidity measurement
18. cwt	h. ____		in the work cited
19. x	i. ____		master of arts
20. CPI	j. ____		namely

Section Three

21. et al.	a. ____		before meals
22. q.h.	b. ____		electrocardiography
23. b.d.	c. ____		gram
24. gt	d. ____		dead on arrival
25. gr	e. ____		distilled water
26. doa	f. ____		every hour
27. g	g. ____		one drop
28. a.c.	h. ____		and others
29. aq. dest.	i. ____		grain
30. EKG	j. ____		twice a day

Corn is as comfortable under the snow as an old man is under his fur coat.
—Russian proverb

41 ©

Section Four

31.	A.D.	a. ____	root mean square
32.	RF	b. ____	and the following
33.	Interpol	c. ____	Kelvin scale, temperature
34.	od	d. ____	also known as
35.	a.k.a.	e. ____	blood factor
36.	et seq.	f. ____	radio frequency
37.	Rh	g. ____	trinitrotoluol
38.	TNT	h. ____	International Criminal Police Organization
39.	rms	i. ____	in the year of our Lord
40.	K	j. ____	outside diameter

Section Five

41.	a.m.	a. ____	messieurs
42.	etc.	b. ____	degree, Celsius
43.	ca.	c. ____	baud
44.	MM.	d. ____	that is
45.	O.D.	e. ____	and so forth
46.	Bd	f. ____	shilling
47.	s	g. ____	nurse
48.	C	h. ____	doctor of optometry
49.	R.N.	i. ____	before noon
50.	i.e.	j. ____	about

Section Six

51.	Tps.	a. ____	which see
52.	dB	b. ____	in the next month
53.	Q.E.D.	c. ____	the current month
54.	N.B.	d. ____	townships
55.	q.v.	e. ____	for the time being
56.	ult.	f. ____	what was to be demonstrated
57.	inst.	g. ____	at the place
58.	pro tem.	h. ____	last month
59.	prox.	i. ____	decibel
60.	ad loc.	j. ____	not well

There is a theory which states that if ever anyone discovers
exactly what the universe is for and why it is here, it will instantly disappear
and be replaced by something even more bizarre and inexplicable.
There is another which states that this has already happened.
—Douglas Adams

Compound Words

Select the most correct word(s) to complete the following sentences.

1. When modems (a. b) there is a (c. d) in information transfer.
   a. breakdown
   b. break down
   c. breakdown
   d. break down
   _____

2. At the (a. b) of the accident, traffic came to a (c. d)
   a. cite
   b. site
   c. standstill
   d. stand still
   _____

3. The next time you're in Denver, let's plan to (a. b) again.
   a. get-together
   b. get together
   _____

4. Mary says that Varina always takes both the (a, b) view.
   a. long- and short-term
   b. long and short-term
   _____

5. For the (a, b) this week the judge sentenced a (c, d) offender.
   a. first-time
   b. first time
   c. first-time
   d. first time
   _____

6. The police are looking for (a, b) stole the folder containing the (c, d) stocks.
   a. whoever
   b. who ever
   c. over-the-counter
   d. over the counter
   _____

7. The latest statistics show that the economy is making a slow (a, b).
   a. turnaround
   b. turn around
   _____

8. Ronald needed logarithm tables to (a, b) the new equations.
   a. resolve
   b. re-solve
   _____

9. (a, b) became (c, d) on the (e, f) flight.
   a. Nobody
   b. No body
   c. airsick
   d. air-sick
   e. New York-Atlanta-Houston
   f. New York, Atlanta, Houston
   _____

10. Those who (a, b) of high school have fewer job opportunities.
    a. dropout
    b. drop out
    _____

11. When the (a, b) became vacant, all the candidates were former (c, d).
    a. vice-presidency
    b. vice presidency
    c. vice-presidents
    d. vice presidents
    _____

12. The article is (a, b), but it still needs (c, d).
    a. up-to-date
    b. up to date
    c. going-over
    d. going over
    _____

43 ©

13. During the (a, b,) period many (d, e) activities were resumed.
    a. post-World War II   b. post World War-II   ____
    c. nongovernmental   d. non-governmental

14. We have the (a, b) to design furnaces that will not discharge (c,d)
    a. know-how   b. know how   ____
    c. carbon-monoxide   d. carbon monoxide
       and sulfur-dioxide   and sulfur dioxide

15. The winning baseball team congratulated (a, b) for their (c, d) victory.
    a. each other   b. one another   ____
    c. come-from-behind   d. come from behind

16. Richard's comments were (a, b) during the (c, d) session.
    a. off-the-record   b. off the record   ____
    c. closed-door   d. closed door

17. Ike said this was an (a, b) case.
    a. open-and-shut   b. open and shut   ____

18. Harry's (a, b) estimation of our (c, d) earnings used the new (e, f)
    software program to develop a strategy that was (g. h).
    a. down-to-earth   b. down to earth   ____
    c. before-tax   d. before tax
    e. state-of-the-art   f. state of the art
    g. well-thought-out   h. well thought out

19. The decision to make an (a. b.) statement was made at a (c. d.).
    a. off-the-record   b. off the record   ____
    c. high-level   d. high level

20. In the usual (a, b) fashion the new (c, d) appliance was quickly
    accepted.
    a. time honored   b. time-honored   ____
    c. timesaving   d. time-saving

21. The (a, b) arrived when the (c, d) of the (e, f) atomic energy project
    began his lecture on the fission of (g, h).
    a. eagerly-awaited moment   b. eagerly awaited moment   ____
    c. ex-president   d. expresident
    e. large-scale   f. large scale
    g. uranium-235   h. Uranium 235

22. John stood (a, b) in the hot sun, but soon became (c, d).
    a. bareheaded   b. bare-headed   ____
    c. sun-burned   d. sunburned

23. This is an (a, b) company engaged in buying (c, d) for the (e,f) North
    Carolina market.
    a. eleven-year-old   b. eleven year old   ____
    c. goat, sheep, and calfskins   d. goat, sheep, and calf skins
    e. Winston-Salem,   f. Winston Salem,

24. (a, b) Warren's writings contain many (c, d) sentences. But (e, f) I
    discuss it with him, he only says, (g, h).
    a. Sometimes   b. Some times   ____
    c. run-on   d. run on
    e. anytime   f. any time
    g. "Alright"   h. "All right"

25. Calvin was (a, b) his ailment was treatable by (c, d).
    a. assured   b. ensured   ____
    c. X-ray   d. X ray

26. FIFO is the (a, b) method of accounting.
    a. first-in-first-out   b. first-in, first-out   ____

27. When the chemical (a, b) is dissolved in water, it remains (c, d).
    a. D.D.T.   b. DDT   ____
    c. unionized   d. un-ionized

28. As Martha sat in traffic which stood (a, b), she rehearsed her (c, d)
    speech on the budget cuts which would be (e, f).
    a. bumper-to-bumper   b. bumper to bumper   ____
    c. after-dinner   d. after dinner
    e. across-the-board   f. across the board

29. Our (a, b) plans include a (c, d) sales campaign and a personal interview
    with our buyers as a (e, f) to these (g, h) objectives.
    a. long-range   b. long range   ____
    c. low-key   d. low key
    e. follow-up   f. follow up
    g. clearly-defined   h. clearly defined

30. Our company demands we list a (a, b) phone number.
    a. day-and-nighttime   b. day- and nighttime   ____

31. The campground was run as a (a, b) operation.
    a. mom-and-pop   b. mom and pop   ____

32. Grace's (a, b) pay barely covered the (c, b) payments on her (e, f) store.
    a. take-home   b. take home   ____
    c. 15-year mortgage   d. 15 year mortgage
    e. Potsdam, New York-based f. Potsdam, New York based

45 ©

33. Chester's (a, b) feeling led him to award a (c, d) loan to the (e, f) (g, h) subsidiary of B.P.
    a. pro-British   b. pro British   ____
    c. long-term   d. long term
    e. wholly-owned   f. wholly owned
    g. worldwide   h. world wide

34. After a (a. b.) trial, his lawyer told the press that it was an (c.d.) case.
    a. long-and-tiring   b. long and tiring   ____
    c. open-and-shut   d. open and shut

35. All (a, b) employees are considered (c, d) (e, f).
    a. per-diem   b. per diem   ____
    c. bona-fide   d. bona fide
    e. independent-contractors f. independent contractors

36. Andrew enjoyed acting as the (a, b) greeter at all our functions.
    a. semi-official   b. semiofficial   ____

37. Colette, a (a, b), has an office in the (c. d) which allows her to watch the (e, f) prices fluctuate.
    a. stockbroker   b. stock broker   ____
    c. stockexchange   d. stock exchange
    e. stockmarket   f. stock market

38. Barry, whose views were considered to be (a, b), was supported by (c, d) (e, f) political groups.
    a. ultraconservative   b. ultra-conservative   ____
    c. like-minded   d. like minded
    e. ultra-active   f. ultra active

39. Jimmy Carter, the (a, b), ended his term with (c, d) memories.
    a. ex-president   b. former president   ____
    c. bitter-sweet   d. bittersweet

When little things would irk me, and I grow
Impatient with my dear ones, make me know
How in a moment joy can take its flight
And happiness be quenched in endless night.
Keep this thought with me all the livelong day
That I may guard the harsh words I might say
When I would fret and grumble, fiery hot,
At trifles that tomorrow are forgot—
Let me remember, Lord, how it would be
If these, my loved ones, were not here with me.
—Author Unknown

46 ©

Pairs of Spelling Errors

Each group of four words contains <u>two</u> spelling errors. Select and correct both misspelled words. Use a dictionary and thesaurus for your answers and to learn the definition, synonyms, and antonyms for any word with which you are unfamiliar.

1. a. supranumerery   ____
   b. buses
   c. vitrious
   d. mustache

2. a. jettison   ____
   b. innoccuous
   c. mocassin
   d. offal

3. a. debacle   ____
   b. melange
   c. ascultation
   d. regim

4. a. anthrapoid   ____
   b. hypocricy
   c. epilogue
   d. accursed

5. a. ax   ____
   b. caliper
   c. harrassment
   d. orbitting

6. a. electicism   ____
   b. imperiled
   c. plebescite
   d. fledgling

7. a. variegated   ____
   b. abismal
   c. provenance
   d. chassi

8. a. paleantology   ____
   b. sepculchre
   c. queue
   d. theater

9. a. worrysome   ____
   b. druggist
   c. flammable
   d. inevitible

10. a. idiosyncrasy   ____
    b. perogative
    c. scurrilous
    d. surveillence

11. a. emolliant   ____
    b. transcendent
    c. penicilin
    d. paraffin

12. a. mischievious   ____
    b. ailimentary
    c. sumptuary
    d. encumbrance

13. a. misanthrope   ____
    b. exhillaration
    c. quizes
    d. conceive

14. a. promissary   ____
    b. maneuver
    c. langorous
    d. mysticism

15. a. gerrymander   ____
    b. priviledge
    c. diaphragm
    d. justapose

16. a. appellent   ____
    b. pneumonia
    c. labeled
    d. quarelled

17. a. calorie   _____   26. a. phlegm   _____
     b. encumberance   b. respirtory
     c. noncommital   c. veterenary
     d. dinghy   d. omniscience

18. a. catharsas   _____   27. a. parenthesis   _____
     b. palpitate   b. mathmatics
     c. relevent   c. demeanor
     d. mileage   d. intervenously

19. a. knowledgeable   _____   28. a. nemises   _____
     b. penchent   b. quixotic
     c. unannimous   c. aegis
     d. tendency   d. Sisiphean

20. a. serendipity   _____   29. a. ossification   _____
     b. boycot   b. anorexia nervosa
     c. chortle   c. savana
     d. martinette   d. paronoia

21. a. ambrosia   30. a. libreto   _____
     b. enterpreneur   _____   b. collage

     c. tarrif   c. fiftyeth
     d. glyph   d. caricature

22. a. affadafit   _____   31. a. toccata   _____
     b. waiver   b. suite
     c. rescesion   c. pointilism
     d. lien   d. opereta

23. a. consumerism   _____   32. a. coloquiallism   _____
     b. proletariet   b. hyperbole
     c. subpoena   c. zenophobia
     d. embezzlment   d. euphemism

24. a. suretax   _____   33. a. denoument   _____
     b. proprietorship   b. oxymoron
     c. appeasment   c. alliteration
     d. vendor   d. soliloquey

25. a. deterance   _____   34. a. plagarism   _____
     b. bicameral   b. allegory
     c. ethnocentric   c. synonimous
     d. hegemany   d. animosity

35. a. mores   ____
    b. nihilism
    c. holacaust
    d. rapprochment

36. a. recidivism   ____
    b. aculturation
    c. medievil
    d. sedition

37. a. plebicite   ____
    b. renaissance
    c. ballistics
    d. carcinnogin

38. a. chromosome   ____
    b. cryogenics
    c. dissalination
    d. ebulient

39. a. equinoc   ____
    b. immunology
    c. metamorphosis
    d. melannin

40. a. perihelion   ____
    b. stallagmite
    c. clarevoyance
    d. transistor

41. a. isicle   ____
    b. mandating
    c. ilusory
    d. Freudian

42. a. Caesarian section   ____
    b. aneckdotal
    c. hemiplegia
    d. kakhi

43. a. calliope   ____
    b. mausolium
    c. salmonella
    d. novacain

44. a. laditude   ____
    b. picknicked
    c. salubrious
    d. engagement

45. a. anniversary   ____
    b. callypso
    c. acceed
    d. hurricane

46. a. waifer   ____
    b. waylayed
    c. devious
    d. abhorrence

47. a. Chattenooga   ____
    b. exhilaration
    c. digestable
    d. encephalitis

48. a. kerosene   ____
    b. intersede
    c. maleable
    d. mandated

49. a. Alzheimer's Disease   ____
    b. fungicidal
    c. trillogy
    d. feacundity

50. a. surveillance   ____
    b. apocryphal
    c. sophmore
    d. ideosyncratic

51. a. antepodes   ____
    b. Appalachin
    c. Biloxi
    d. climactic

52. a. Terre-Haut   ____
    b. laryngitis
    c. mutinere
    d. mercurial

53. a. painfull   ____   60. a. rhapsody   ____
    b. lionharted   b. halfhazard
    c. Chianti   c. sojourn
    d. bacchanal   d. Albuequerque

54. a. guillotine   ____   61. a. Tuscon   ____
    b. magesterial   b. somersault
    c. moribound   c. amethyst
    d. Bosc pears   d. mertricious

55. a. Cleveland   ____   62. a. Saskachewan   ____
    b. catarr   b. Braille
    c. malocclusion   c. parlimentary
    d. ascerbate   d. candidacy

56. a. citidal   ____   63. a. coterie   ____
    b. somber   b. Millwaukee
    c. greeddiness   c. comtrollor
    d. Eiffel Tower   d. doctrinaire

57. a. catagorical   ____   64. a. formaldehyde   ____
    b. mayonaise   b. contamacious
    c. libelous   c. lariat
    d. saccharide   d. hallilujah

58. a. torturous   ____   65. a. pirouette   ____
    b. Missourri   b. seder
    c. zodiack   c. convalesence
    d. emeritus   d. Minneapolus

59. a. Pennsyllviana   ____   66. a. pheasant   ____
    b. tourniquet   b. Ammarilo
    c. barbique   c. vaccination
    d. limousine   d. desicrate

God's Minute

I have only just one minute.
Only sixty seconds in it.
Forced upon me — can't refuse it,
Didn't seek it, didn't choose it.
But it's up to me to use it.
I must suffer if I loose it.
Give account if I abuse it.
Just a tiny little minute ...
But eternity is in it.
—Anonymous

CHAPTER 3: SYNONYMS and ANTONYMS

Synonym Matching Columns

Fill in the blank with the number of the synonym. Write an **antonym** for each numbered word in the space provided on the right.

Section One

1. ebullient	a. ____ to polish	_____
2. propensity	b. ____ harbinger	_____
3. precursor	c. ____ make unnecessary	_____
4. heterodoxy	d. ____ overenthusiastic	_____
5. epistle	e. ____ corresponding	_____
6. adulterate	f. ____ written communication	_____
7. obviate	g. ____ antisocial	_____
8. burnish	h. ____ heresy	_____
9. congruent	i. ____ depreciate	_____
10. misanthropic	j. ____ preference	_____

Section Two

11. intractable	a. ____ period between two successive governments	_____
12. dichotomy	b. ____ not talkative	_____
13. endemic	c. ____ unmanageable	_____
14. taciturn	d. ____ pretend	_____
15. macerate	e. ____ eulogy	_____
16. encomium	f. ____ division into two parts	_____
17. interregnum	g. ____ deviating from a rule	_____
18. anomaly	h. ____ fringe benefit	_____
19. feign	i. ____ soften by soaking	_____
20. perquisite	j. ____ belonging to a specific place	_____

Section Three

21. coagulate	a. ____ dizziness	_____
22. moribund	b. ____ humorous in an odd way	_____
23. extrapolate	c. ____ nonconformist	_____
24. vertigo	d. ____ overwhelming	_____
25. castigate	e. ____ congeal	_____
26. droll	f. ____ avoid	_____
27. insuperable	g. ____ dying out	_____
28. eschew	h. ____ winding	_____
29. tortuous	i. ____ severely criticize	_____
30. iconoclast	j. ____ project a trend	_____

Section Four

31. nonplus	a. ____ omnipresent	_____
32. complaisant	b. ____ trivia	_____
33. indomitable	c. ____ inelegant	_____
34. immutable	d. ____ admirable	_____
35. minutiae	e. ____ many edges	_____
36. dilettante	f. ____ obliging	_____
37. gauche	g. ____ unchanging	_____
38. serrated	h. ____ amateur	_____
39. ubiquitous	i. ____ unconquerable	_____
40. exemplary	j. ____ confuse	_____

Section Five

41. captious	a. ____ extreme poverty	_____
42. histrionic	b. ____ weaken	_____
43. martial	c. ____ embarrassing social error	_____
44. penury	d. ____ hypercritical	_____
45. incorrigible	e. ____ blend of different things	_____
46. emend	f. ____ warlike	_____
47. debilitate	g. ____ temporary suspension	_____
48. abeyance	h. ____ correct	_____
49. gaffe	i. ____ theatrical	_____
50. amalgam	j. ____ unmanageable	_____

Section Six

51. verdant	a. ____ consistent	_____
52. synopsis	b. ____ minor offense	_____
53. puissant	c. ____ cut out	_____
54. tendentious	d. ____ green with vegetation	_____
55. peccadillo	e. ____ defamation	_____
56. aspersion	f. ____ powerful	_____
57. extirpate	g. ____ assert	_____
58. burgeon	h. ____ outline	_____
59. aver	i. ____ biased	_____
60. commensurate	j. ____ expand	_____

I believe that anyone can conquer fear by doing the things he fears to do,
provided he keeps doing them until he gets a record of successful
experiences behind him.
—Eleanor Roosevelt

Section Seven

61.	supplant	a. ____	parody	_____
62.	devolve	b. ____	fissure	_____
63.	rift	c. ____	sympathize with	_____
64.	nostrum	d. ____	replace	_____
65.	commiserate	e. ____	proclivity	_____
66.	elucidate	f. ____	force	_____
67.	burlesque	g. ____	remedy	_____
68.	coerce	h. ____	humorous misuse of a word	_____
69.	malapropism	i. ____	to pass on	_____
70.	predilection	j. ____	explain	_____

Section Eight

71.	pan	a. ____	abundance	_____
72.	perfunctory	b. ____	wary	_____
73.	chary	c. ____	disappear	_____
74.	estrange	d. ____	find fault	_____
75.	cornucopia	e. ____	meddlesome	_____
76.	lassitude	f. ____	unenthusiastic	_____
77.	resound	g. ____	overweight	_____
78.	abscond	h. ____	alienate	_____
79.	corpulent	i. ____	reverberate	_____
80.	officious	j. ____	weakness	_____

Section Nine

81.	regimen	a. ____	thick and sticky	_____
82.	equanimity	b. ____	threatening	_____
83.	viscous	c. ____	regulated course of treatment	_____
84.	inimical	d. ____	uncommonly gifted	_____
85.	baleful	e. ____	cause delay through indecision	_____
86.	quasi	f. ____	accuse	_____
87.	temporize	g. ____	calm	_____
88.	precocious	h. ____	equivalent	_____
89.	impeach	i. ____	resembling	_____
90.	tantamount	j. ____	unfavorable	_____

We have not lost faith, but we have transferred it from God
to the medical profession. —George Bernard Shaw

Section Ten

91. panegyric
92. suffuse
93. warrant
94. demur
95. apposite
96. dispassionate
97. compunction
98. jocular
99. ribald
100. ancillary

a. ____ vulgar
b. ____ remorse
c. ____ subordinate
d. ____ tribute
e. ____ justify
f. ____ fond of joking
g. ____ overspread
h. ____ pertinent
i. ____ to take exception
j. ____ impartial

Section Eleven

101. arrears
102. sententious
103. titular
104. cursory
105. benighted
106. ineluctable
107. purblind
108. bathos
109. importune
110. cache

a. ____ in name only
b. ____ hiding place
c. ____ unpaid debts
d. ____ slow in understanding
e. ____ false pathos
f. ____ concise
g. ____ ignorant
h. ____ urge with annoying persistence
i. ____ superficial
j. ____ unavoidable

Section Twelve

111. effete
112. benign
113. venal
114. diverse
115. palpitate
116. absurd
117. primitive
118. pungent
119. arbiter
120. malevolent

a. ____ showing ill will
b. ____ ludicrous
c. ____ acrid
d. ____ beat rapidly
e. ____ judge
f. ____ differing
g. ____ kindly
h. ____ corrupt
i. ____ decadent
j. ____ aboriginal

Habit is habit, and not to be flung out of the window,
but coaxed downstairs one step at a time.
—Mark Twain

54 ©

Section Thirteen

121.	permeate	a. ____ highest point		_____
122.	retroflex	b. ____ talkative		_____
123.	ambulatory	c. ____ off hand		_____
124.	pallid	d. ____ enmity		_____
125.	voluble	e. ____ refuse scornfully		_____
126.	rancor	f. ____ marriage relationship		_____
127.	disdain	g. ____ bent backwards		_____
128.	conjugal	h. ____ wan		_____
129.	apogee	i. ____ able to walk		_____
130.	cavalier	j. ____ diffuse		_____

Section Fourteen

131.	coalesce	a. ____ trite remark		_____
132.	fecund	b. ____ concise		_____
133.	interim	c. ____ stipulation		_____
134.	redundant	d. ____ blend together		_____
135.	malleable	e. ____ repay		_____
136.	taboo	f. ____ prolific		_____
137.	terse	g. ____ repetitious		_____
138.	platitude	h. ____ forbidden		_____
139.	requite	i. ____ pliable		_____
140.	proviso	j. ____ temporary		_____

Life can only be understood backwards.
It must be lived forwards.
—Soren Kierkegaard

The growth of the human mind is still high adventure,
in many ways the highest adventure on earth.
—Norman Cousins

Man must evolve for all human conflict a method which rejects revenge,
aggression and retaliation.
The foundation of such a method is love.
—Martin Luther King, Jr.

The air plane stays up because it doesn't have time to fall.
—Orville Wright, 1903

Antonym Matching Columns

Fill in the blanks with the number of the antonym. Write a **synonym** for each numbered word in the space provided on the right. Synonym answers can be found in Answer Key #2.

Section One

1. zealot	a. ____ simple	1. _____
2. satiate	b. ____ equality	2. _____
3. nepotism	c. ____ dependent	3. _____
4. autonomous	d. ____ consistent	4. _____
5. jocund	e. ____ clarify	5. _____
6. obfuscate	f. ____ indifferent	6. _____
7. candor	g. ____ melancholy	7. _____
8. disparity	h. ____ impartiality	8. _____
9. capricious	i. ____ frustrate	9. _____
10. baroque	j. ____ subtlety	10. _____

Section Two

11. choleric	a. ____ summery	11. _____
12. assuage	b. ____ urbanized	12. _____
13. hibernal	c. ____ recalcitrant	13. _____
14. evanescent	d. ____ continued	14. _____
15. obloquy	e. ____ witty	15. _____
16. sanguine	f. ____ serene	16. _____
17. amenable	g. ____ praise	17. _____
18. fatuous	h. ____ irritate	18. _____
19. bucolic	i. ____ gloomy	19. _____
20. discrete	j. ____ permanent	20. _____

Section Three

21. garrulous	a. ____ cadaverous	21. _____
22. excoriate	b. ____ definite	22. _____
23. untenable	c. ____ accurate	23. _____
24. tyro	d. ____ precise	24. _____
25. catholic	e. ____ supportable	25. _____
26. amorphous	f. ____ duplicity	26. _____
27. equivocal	g. ____ praise	27. _____
28. obese	h. ____ expert	28. _____
29. probity	i. ____ narrow	29. _____
30. fallacious	j. ____ taciturn	30. _____

You can know something in your brain, but you don't really know it
until you know it in your bones. —Anonymous

56 ©

Synonym Sentences

Select the word(s) that most nearly defines the underlined word in each sentence.   Use a thesaurus and dictionary to write one synonym for the four choices in each question.

1. He acted in the most <u>delusory</u> manner.
    a. faultless
    b. fallacious
    c. respectable
    d. suitable

2. Margie was asked to <u>corroborate</u> the plaintiff's testimony.
    a. pervert
    b. abate
    c. suborn
    d. affirm

3. The unexpected <u>charity</u> shown by the usually obdurate judge overwhelmed the prisoner.
    a. magnanimity
    b. parsimony
    c. deprecation
    d. orotundity

4. There were caught trying to sell a <u>spurious</u> Roman statue.
    a. fraudulent
    b. authentic
    c. desultory
    d. legitimate

5. He remained an <u>errant</u> traveller all his life.
    a. spurious
    b. meandering
    c. imperfect
    d. enigmatic

6. I would like <u>to tender</u> a suggestion to the committee.
    a. debate
    b. retract
    c. proffer
    d. forestall

7. A <u>variant</u> spelling of Smith is Smythe.
    a. intrinsic
    b. divergent
    c. plagiarized
    d. pointless

8. <u>Requital</u> must be made for her loss.
    a. Application
    b. Enforcement
    c. Requisite
    d. Compensation

9. The law students were asked to discuss a <u>hypothetical</u> case on contract law in class.
    a. deceitful
    b. suppositional
    c. substantive
    d. discordant

10. In the <u>previous</u> paragraph Chris was named the executor of the will.
    a. antecedent
    b. subsequent
    c. antecedence
    d. ensuing

11. Out of <u>deference</u> to his high official standing, the rules committee acquiesced.
    a. contempt
    b. contumacy
    c. default
    d. respect

12. Lena considered herself to be a <u>connoisseur</u> of Danish cheese.
    a. dilettante
    b. consumer
    c. gourmand
    d. cognoscente

13. Such <u>heinous</u> acts cannot be tolerated; we must find the culprits.
    a. reprehensible
    b. meritorious
    c. chaotic
    d. perfunctory

14. The <u>opprobrium</u> of his actions followed him to the grave.
    a. esteem
    b. acceptance
    c. disapprobation
    d. cynicism

By perseverance the snail reached the ark.
—Charles Haddon Spurgeon

15. The candidate continually <u>impugned</u> the motives of his opponent.
    a. assailed   ____
    b. advocated
    c. supported
    d. ascribed

16. The city council held a <u>conclave</u> before the scheduled meeting.
    a. discussion group   ____
    b. agreement
    c. open gathering
    d. private assembly

17. Many felt that this argument was <u>tenuous</u>.
    a. valid   ____
    b. unsubstantial
    c. phlegmatic
    d. timid

18. The debate team argued its position in a <u>trenchant</u> manner.
    a. disorganized   ____
    b. rambling
    c. incisive
    d. mordant

19. His <u>scurrilous</u> remarks were quoted in the minutes of the meeting.
    a. refined   ____
    b. agreeable
    c. unpublished
    d. derogatory

20. The judge called the complainant a <u>vexatious</u> litigant.
    a. habitual   ____
    b. troublesome
    c. understanding
    d. talkative

Life is like playing a violin in public and learning
the instrument as one goes on.
—Samuel Butler

You've got to be very careful if you don't know where you are going,
because you might not get there.
—Yogi Berra

59 ©

Selecting Antonyms

Select the word which has the <u>opposite</u> meaning. Use a thesaurus and dictionary to write at least one **synonym** for the five words in each group.

1. alleviate   ____   8. amalgamate   ____
   a. succor   a. separate
   b. worsen   b. commingle
   c. temper   c. alloy
   d. assuage   d. surprise

2. obsequious   ____   9. salubrious   ____
   a. menial   a. therapeutic
   b. assertive   b. unctuous
   c. ingratiating   c. harmful
   d. perceptive   d. inoffensive

3. antipathy   ____   10. infinite   ____
   a. aversion   a. interminable
   b. memorable   b. bounded
   c. affinity   c. debilitate
   d. enmity   d. adroit

4. abase   ____   11. loquacious   ____
   a. vitiate   a. taciturn
   b. humble   b. voluble
   c. renounce   c. prolix
   d. elevate   d. sonorous

5. obtuse   ____   12. phlegmatic   ____
   a. acute   a. nonchalant
   b. dull   b. droll
   c. diffident   c. animated
   d. archaic   d. rogue

6. abide   ____   13. penury   ____
   a. taper   a. affluence
   b. dissipate   b. impoverishment
   c. encumber   c. impertinent
   d. depart   d. forfeit

7. opprobrious   ____   14. inculcate   ____
   a. praising   a. imbue
   b. censorious   b. augment
   c. improvident   c. learn
   d. negativistic   d. curtail

60 ©

15. disparity
a. contrast
b. serene
c. allotment
d. harmony

_____ 23. indigenous
a. aboriginal
b. sympathetic
c. somnolent
d. foreign

_____

16. dormant
a. asymptomatic
b. quiescent
c. animated
d. encouraged

_____ 24. debilitate
a. enervate
b. enlighten
c. abate
d. invigorate

_____

17. bombastic
a. temperate
b. turgid
c. gauche
d. audacious

_____ 25. captious
a. censorious
b. perverse
c. laudatory
d. unwavering

_____

18. ingenuous
a. artless
b. spontaneous
c. maladroit
d. sophisticated

_____ 26. vindicate
a. exonerate
b. contradict
c. relent
d. exculpate

_____

19. asperity
a. acrimony
b. affability
c. surliness
d. roughness

_____ 27. retrospective
a. reminiscence
b. residual
c. afterthought
d. impetuous

_____

20. vestige
a. leftover
b. no evidence
c. souvenir
d. maximize

_____ 28. morose
a. despondent
b. waning
c. genial
d. somber

_____

21. rectify
a. compensate
b. redeem
c. worsen
d. alive

_____ 29. redundant
a. essential
b. superfluous
c. dispensable
d. crude

_____

22. perfunctory
a. cursory
b. apathetic
c. diligent
d. omnivorous

_____ 30. covetous
a. avaricious
b. mercenary
c. surreptitious
d. bountiful

_____

Antonyms

In each group of four words select the <u>two</u> words that are most nearly opposite in meaning. Use a dictionary and a thesaurus to learn the definition, synonym, and antonym for any word with which you are unfamiliar.

1. a. disagreeable   ____
    b. propitious
    c. stalemate
    d. stagger

2. a. egress   ____
    b. temerity
    c. entry
    d. progression

3. a. competition   ____
    b. manifest
    c. latter
    d. initial

4. a. prolific   ____
    b. mature
    c. demagogue
    d. callow

5. a. stalwart   ____
    b. banter
    c. timorous
    d. affectation

6. a. concession   ____
    b. propagation
    c. stimulus
    d. denial

7. a. appendix   ____
    b. historical
    c. assistance
    d. introductory material

8. a. indulge   ____
    b. validate
    c. annul
    d. intolerant

9. a. acolyte   ____
    b. wiles
    c. candor
    d. bankrupt

10. a. esteemed   ____
    b. controversy
    c. dormant
    d. trivial

11. a. agreeable   ____
    b. tortuous
    c. gratifying
    d. direct

12. a. dispassionate   ____
    b. emissary
    c. emotional
    d. categorical

13. a. malcontent   ____
    b. malignant
    c. complacent
    d. pernicious

14. a. predispose   ____
    b. pragmatic
    c. theoretical
    d. predominant

15. a. salubrious   ____
    b. postulate
    c. deleterious
    d. subtract

16. a. discretion   ____
    b. catabolic
    c. cataclysm
    d. temerity

Personally I'm always ready to learn, although
I do not always like being taught. —Winston Churchill

17. a. kaleidoscopic   ____
    b. fanaticism
    c. secondary
    d. skepticism

18. a. possibility   ____
    b. ordinary
    c. opprobrious
    d. ethical

19. a. conciliate   ____
    b. accommodate
    c. aloof
    d. gregarious

20. a. corporeal   ____
    b. bland
    c. corporal
    d. caustic

21. a. avocation   ____
    b. occupation
    c. good
    d. stimulation

22. a. congeal   ____
    b. fractious
    c. liquefy
    d. recalcitrant

23. a. febrile   ____
    b. cursory
    c. luminescence
    d. profound

24. a. pedantic   ____
    b. pompous
    c. pliant
    d. inflexible

25. a. shun   ____
    b. enemy
    c. agency
    d. fraternize

26. a. urbane   ____
    b. municipal
    c. munificent
    d. tactless

27. a. zephyr   ____
    b. zenith
    c. verve
    d. nadir

28. a. variance   ____
    b. discrepancy
    c. encompass
    d. exclude

29. a. singular   ____
    b. wallow
    c. collective
    d. flounder

30. a. decision   ____
    b. twine
    c. triplet
    d. stalemate

31. a. ephemeral   ____
    b. everlasting
    c. abundant
    d. stoppage

32. a. repetitious   ____
    b. reticent
    c. subsequent
    d. prior

33. a. bizarre   ____
    b. gelid
    c. torrid
    d. oriental

34. a. alleviate   ____
    b. paragon
    c. aggravate
    d. voracious

Professionals built the *Titanic*; amateurs, the ark. —Author Unknown

63 ©

35. a. redundant
    b. contrite
    c. prolix
    d. impenitent   ____

36. a. inherent
    b. derision
    c. extrinsic
    d. sham   ____

37. a. magisterial
    b. plebeian
    c. surfeit
    d. plane   ____

38. a. transpire
    b. demure
    c. untranslatable
    d. impudent   ____

39. a. granulate
    b. recalcitrant
    c. tractable
    d. crystallize   ____

40. a. extirpate
    b. exculpate
    c. indict
    d. amend   ____

41. a. erudite
    b. vigorous
    c. languid
    d. experienced   ____

42. a. proclivity
    b. tendency
    c. ebullient
    d. placid   ____

43. a. estranged
    b. reconciled
    c. subsequently
    d. factually   ____

44. a. turgid
    b. harass
    c. hapless
    d. fortunate   ____

45. a. candid
    b. panacea
    c. cryptic
    d. cupidity   ____

46. a. plethora
    b. inappropriate
    c. inhibit
    d. apposite   ____

Perhaps the most valuable result of all education is the ability
to make yourself do the thing you have to do, when it ought to be done,
whether you like it or not.
—Thomas Henry Huxley

Courage is master of fear, not absence of fear.
—Mark Twain

I seldom think about my limitations, and they never make me sad.
Perhaps there is just a touch of yearning at times;
but it is vague, like a breeze among flowers.
—Helen Keller

Synonyms and Antonyms using Analogy

Each question below consists of a pair of words that are either synonyms or antonyms to each other. This pair is followed by another word related to the four selections below by analogy. Select the correct word and indicate if the meanings are similar (synonym) ordissimilar (antonym).

Example:

Redundant is to superfluous as litigation is to
  a. lawsuit *   c. publication
  b. argument   d. dissertation

Redundant is a synonym of superfluous, therefore the answer will be a synonym of litigation: lawsuit.   Answer: a. - synonym

1.   Abate is to reduction as accuse is to
        a. plea   c. blame
        b. reply   d. vindicate   _____

2.   Abominate is to admire as altruism is to
        a. beneficence   c. astound
        b. misanthropy   d. tolerance   _____

3.   Frugal is to parsimonious as prodigal is to
        a. meager   c. provident
        b. large   d. profligate   _____

4.   Ravenous is to sated as insipid is to
        a. stimulating   c. gentle
        b. banal   d. prosaic   _____

5.   Gastronomy is to epicure as malign is to
        a. extol   c. eulogize
        b. abuse   d. benign   _____

6.   Professedly is to ostensibly as abettor is to
        a. dissuader   c. advocator
        b. exposer   d. gambler   _____

7.   Impeccable is to irreproachable as duplicity is to
        a. guile   c. frail
        b. candor   d. doubling   _____

8.   Decorum is to impropriety as provincial is to
        a. local   c. governmental
        b. bucolic   d. urbane   _____

9. Panacea is to elixir as meretricious is to
    a. legitimate   c. specious
    b. efficacious   d. worthy   _____

10. Effigy is to representation as fastidious is to
    a. meticulous   c. quick
    b. indulgent   d. squeamish   _____

11. Abstemious is to hedonism as concave is to
    a. sunken   c. indented
    b. convex   d. broken   _____

12. Equivocate is to truth-telling as salubrious is to
    a. salutary   c. miasmic
    b. rustic   d. deleterious   _____

13. Questioning is to inquisitive as facetious is to
    a. factious   c. jocular
    b. lugubrious   d. serious   _____

14. Sub rosa is to openness as untenable is to
    a. spurious   c. groundless
    b. sustained   d. twisting   _____

15. Misprize is to deprecate as refute is to
    a. invalidate   c. substantiate
    b. vindicate   d. prohibit   _____

16. Abjudicate is to decide as adjudicate is to
    a. classify   c. unsettle
    b. disarrange   d. decree   _____

17. Laches is to immediate as palliative is to
    a. beneficial   c. tempering
    b. detrimental   d. sleepy   _____

18. Comity is to discord as ex gratia is to
    a. favor   c. required task
    b. accommodation d. free   _____

19. Despondent is to cheerful as recalcitrant is to
    a. tractable   c. calculating
    b. erratic   d. obstinate   _____

20. Dilatory is to punctual as libel is to
    a. ability   c. vilify
    b. vindication   d. calumny   _____

21. Zealot is to enthusiast as assimilate is to
 a. reject   c. anticipate
 b. integrate   d. segregate
              _____

22. Vacillation is to resolution as peripheral is to
 a. central   c. around
 b. geometric   d. boundary
              _____

23. Illusory is to unreal as exacerbate is to
 a. alleviate   c. question
 b. assuage   d. aggravate
              _____

24. Incongruous is to consistency as unanimity is to
 a. accordance c. discordance
 b. harmoniousness d. ambiguity
              _____

25. Discriminating is to connoisseur as apposite is to
 a. inappropriate c. opposite
 b. pertinent   d. irrelevant
              _____

26. Trepidation is to dauntless as dissonance is to
 a. mellifluous c. silence
 b. apathy   d. raucous
              _____

27. Expertise is to virtuoso as palpable is to
 a. implacable c. tangible
 b. undiscernible d. tremble
              _____

28. Didactic is to teach as abrogate is to
 a. terminate   c. create
 b. sanction   d. diminish
              _____

29. Volatile is to evaporate as equivocate is to
 a. specific   c. explicit
 b. equal   d. ambiguous
              _____

30. Fancy is to whimsical as petite is to
 a. affectionate c. attractive
 b. diminutive   d. reduced
              _____

31. Explicit is to implication as surreptitious is to
 a. accidental   c. overt
 b. clandestine   d. stealthy
              _____

32. Inane is to sense as derisive is to
 a. derive   c. ridicule
 b. neglectful   d. laudatory
              _____

67 ©

33. Propensity is to disinclination as transience is to
    a. permanence   c. changeable
    b. evanescence   d. ephemeral   _____

34. Unimportant is to trivia as compliance is to
    a. disobedience   c. deference
    b. decisiveness   d. assertive   _____

35. Emotion is to dispassionate as inscrutable is to
    a. obvious   c. unwritten
    b. arcane   d. elusive   _____

36. Essential is to incidental as erratic is to
    a. erotic   c. harmful
    b. suspicious   d. stable   _____

37. Haughtiness is to arrogance as avarice is to
    a. generosity   c. benevolence
    b. venality   d. inclination   _____

38. Perception is to discerning as sumptuous is to
    a. partial   c. ordinary
    b. munificent   d. multifarious _____

39. Obstruct is to impede as impenetrable is to
    a. impervious   c. open
    b. hidden   d. accessible   _____

40. Impoverished is to affluent as irascible is to
    a. bellicose   c. rash
    b. placid   d. irritable   _____

41. Corroborate is to invalidate as adamant is to
    a. admittance   c. yielding
    b. primeval   d. inflexible   _____

42. Ingenuous is to sophisticated as audacity is to
    a. bravado   c. hearing
    b. bold   d. cowardice   _____

43. Tenacity is to persistence as fealty is to
    a. anger   c. anxiety
    b. loyalty   d. faith   _____

44. Erudite is to scholarly as adipose is to
    a. fatty   c. liquid
    b. anomaly   d. position   _____

45. Countenance is to prohibition as egregious is to
    a. addition
    b. mistake
    c. moderate
    d. notorious
    _____

46. Exculpate is to exonerate as corpulent is to
    a. rotund
    b. emaciated
    c. corporeal
    d. material
    _____

47. Indigenous is to alien as amorphous is to
    a. opaque
    b. translucent
    c. diaphanous
    d. organized
    _____

48. Cede is to annex as precipitate is to
    a. retard
    b. solute
    c. steep
    d. quicken
    _____

49. Chagrin is to mortification as malfeasance is to
    a. amiable
    b. misconduct
    c. poor performance
    d. seasickness
    _____

50. Clandestine is to open as cohesive is to
    a. detached
    b. affiliated
    c. attached
    d. consolidated
    _____

51. Garrulous is to wordy as chicanery is to
    a. chastity
    b. poultry
    c. penury
    d. trickery
    _____

52. Peremptory is to indecisive as duress is to
    a. flimsy
    b. volition
    c. intimidation
    d. compulsion
    _____

53. Punctilious is to prompt as extortion is to
    a. coercion
    b. denounce
    c. return
    d. denigrate
    _____

54. Chronic is to continual as empiric is to
    a. empire
    b. firsthand
    c. experiential
    d. theoretical
    _____

55. Putative is to alleged as abstruse is to
    a. sagacious
    b. incomprehensible
    c. obvious
    d. superficial
    _____

56. Celibate is to conjugal as somatic is to
    a. physical
    b. frantic
    c. mental
    d. soporific
    _____

57. Discord is to amity as abhor is to
    a. execrate   c. accuse
    b. admire   d. detest   _____

58. Analogous is to comparable as sustain is to
    a. support   c. estimate
    b. refute   d. contravene   _____

59. Atrophy is to development as synthetic is to
    a. fiber   c. viscous
    b. plastic   d. natural   _____

60. Diagnosis is to analysis as spasm is to
    a. cramp   c. erratic
    b. steady   d. inexorable   _____

61. Wanton is to malevolent as premeditated is to
    a. medication   c. impetuous
    b. impulsive   d. prepense   _____

62. Contentious is to pacific as deleterious is to
    a. advantageous   c. detrimental
    b. injurious   d. intentional   _____

63. Provisional is to tentative as plagiarize is to
    a. impede   c. steal ideas
    b. annoy   d. borrow   _____

64. Sedentary is to active as urbanity is to
    a. rusticity   c. suavity
    b. elegance   d. civility   _____

65. Therapeutic is to curative as truncate is to
    a. cancel   c. divide
    b. elongate   d. abridge   _____

66. Disparity is to unequal as intractable is to
    a. submissive   c. obstinate
    b. harmful   d. methodical   _____

God does not play dice with the universe. —Albert Einstein

God not only plays dice, but he also sometimes throws the dice
where they cannot be seen. —Stephen Hawking

Select Antonym or Synonym

Each numbered word has four words listed below it. Select the letter for the word which is most nearly the same as or the opposite of the numbered word. Indicate your letter choice and write an S for synonym or A for antonym. Use a dictionary and a thesaurus for your answers and to learn the definition, synonyms, and antonyms for any word with which you are unfamiliar.

1. pellucid   _____
   a. inherent
   b. limpid
   c. anticipation
   d. obdurate

2. palliate   _____
   a. awry
   b. askew
   c. alleviate
   d. deplore

3. grandiose   _____
   a. exotic
   b. increase
   c. provocative
   d. simple

4. extraneous   _____
   a. stronger
   b. essential
   c. foreigner
   d. augment

5. ennui   _____

   a. auspicious
   b. paucity
   c. excitement
   d. astute

6. solvent   _____
   a. bankrupt
   b. solution
   c. prolific
   d. answer

7. jejune   _____
   a. jingoism
   b. jargon
   c. youthful
   d. jocund

8. criticism   _____
   a. judicial
   b. jurisdiction
   c. approval
   d. lustrous

9. viable   _____
   a. deathly
   b. moribund
   c. macabre
   d. invidious

10. valedictory   _____
    a. harbinger
    b. histrionic
    c. extraneous
    d. salutatory

11. interdict   _____
    a. intervene
    b. introduce
    c. prohibit
    d. dictate

12. ineluctable   _____
    a. expandable
    b. invaluable
    c. irresistible
    d. irascible

71 ©

13. sycophant   _____
    a. synopsis
    b. servile
    c. synonym
    d. psychological

14. talisman   _____
    a. terminology
    b. medicine man
    c. gambler
    d. amulet

15. transient   _____
    a. transparent
    b. transgression
    c. permanent
    d. perfunctory

16. tentative   _____
    a. experimental
    b. tendentious
    c. traumatic
    d. engender

17. spurious   _____
    a. genre
    b. stultify
    c. genuine
    d. soporific

18. prefatory   _____
    a. precocity
    b. epilogue
    c. prophylactic
    d. combative

19. mordant   _____
    a. dying
    b. moratorium
    c. morganatic
    d. sarcastic

20. multilingual   _____
    a. polyglot
    b. multilateral
    c. multiplied
    d. polyandry

21. illusive   _____
    a. hiatus
    b. illustration
    c. funereal
    d. deceiving

22. impalpable   _____
    a. tautological
    b. tangible
    c. impenetrable
    d. implacable

23. magniloquence   _____
    a. diminish
    b. ignoble
    c. extravagance
    d. exalted

24. diurnal   _____
    a. daily
    b. weekly
    c. monthly
    d. yearly

25. unwitting   _____
    a. clever
    b. intentional
    c. brilliant
    d. unintelligent

26. ciliated   _____
    a. square
    b. colorless
    c. coded
    d. hairy

27. execrate   _____
    a. carry out
    b. acclaim
    c. accomplish
    d. assassinate

28. soporific   _____
    a. slow
    b. awakening
    c. quick
    d. caustic

29. inundate   _____
    a. invalidate
    b. inveigh
    c. denote
    d. drain

30. collusion   _____
    a. accident
    b. collaborative
    c. damage
    d. injury

31. extemporaneous   _____
    a. additional
    b. temporal
    c. rhetorical
    d. premeditate

32. asperity   _____
    a. quickness
    b. slow
    c. good temper
    d. beekeeping

33. appease   _____
    a. disrupt
    b. agitate
    c. amass
    d. amplify

34. penchant   _____
    a. amulet
    b. jewel
    c. dislike
    d. aptitude

35. peripatetic   _____
    a. moving
    b. outside
    c. circle
    d. instrument

36. sapient   _____
    a. discerning
    b. sardonic
    c. youthful
    d. unwell

37. orifice   _____
    a. forehead
    b. device
    c. opening
    d. orotund

38. inimical   _____
    a. antagonistic
    b. anonymous
    c. pompous
    d. insipid

39. diffidence   _____
    a. different
    b. malcontent
    c. opposite
    d. boldness

40. centripetal   _____
    a. centrifugal
    b. circumference
    c. medicine
    d. outside

41. celerity   _____
    a. vegetable
    b. delay
    c. happy
    d. festive

42. crescendo   _____
    a. accident
    b. collision
    c. full
    d. diminution

43. vicarious   _____
    a. vigorous
    b. aggressive
    c. substitute
    d. clergy

44. vindictive   _____
    a. win
    b. revenge
    c. absolute
    d. convincing

73 ©

45. virulent   _____   48. germane   _____
    a. malignant   a. Teutonic
    b. strong   b. irrelevant
    c. masculine   c. healthful
    d. feminine   d. microorganism

46. stertorous   _____   49. sophomoric   _____
    a. strong   a. insipid
    b. labored   b. school
    c. lyrical   c. mature
    d. dinosaur   d. fraternity

47. tautology   _____   50. vexatious   _____
    a. tension   a. confusing
    b. loose   b. aligned
    c. study of Greek alphabet   c. annoying
    d. repetition   d. assured

One word Frees us of all the weight and pain of life: That word is love.
—Sophocles 406 B.C.

Learning at its best, is a magical experience. When it's happening,
don't analyze it and try to put it into some educational jargon.
Just dance with it. Enjoy it. Love it.
—Anonymous

Some people have greatness thrust upon them.
Very few have excellence thrust upon them. —John Gardner

I not only use all the brains I have, but all that I can borrow.
—Woodrow Wilson

There is more to life, than increasing its speed.
—Gandhi

If a man does not keep pace with his companions,
perhaps it is because he hears a different drummer.
Let him step to the music he hears,
however measured or far away.
—Henry David Thoreau

Unrelated Words

In each group of four words select the <u>one</u> word that is least similar in meaning or unrelated to the other three words. Write the shared meaning of the related words. Use a dictionary and thesaurus for your answers and to learn the definition, synonyms, and antonyms for any word with which you are unfamiliar.

1. a. congeniality   ____
    b. animosity
    c. enmity
    d. animus

2. a. inflate   ____
    b. distend
    c. dilate
    d. annul

3. a. censorious   ____
    b. fawning
    c. captious
    d. caviling

4. a. circuit   ____
    b. redundant
    c. tautological
    d. circumlocution

5. a. contemn   ____
    b. scorn
    c. esteem
    d. flout

6. a. macerate   ____
    b. smash
    c. pulverize
    d. negligent

7. a. vociferous   ____
    b. duress
    c. obstreperous
    d. clamorous

8. a. saturnine   ____
    b. dour
    c. planetary
    d. surly

9. a. obdurate   ____
    b. implacable
    c. adaptable
    d. adamant

10. a. resonant   ____
    b. innovative
    c. sonorous
    d. orotund

11. a. placid   ____
    b. callow
    c. uncouth
    d. crude

12. a. panache   ____
    b. gusto
    c. zest
    d. apprehension

13. a. temerity   ____
    b. timidity
    c. effrontery
    d. audacity

14. a. discordant   ____
    b. dissonant
    c. terminate
    d. cacophonous

15. a. accessory   ____
    b. parapet
    c. rampart
    d. abutment

16. a. inane   ____
    b. vapid
    c. profound
    d. jejune

17. a. candor   ____   26. a. prodigal   ____
     b. fearless   b. profligate
     c. intrepid   c. spendthrift
     d. dauntless   d. monumental

18. a. vacate   ____   27. a. truculent   ____
     b. quash   b. affable
     c. abrogate   c. bellicose
     d. deliberate   d. belligerent

19. a. transient   ____   28. a. nuptial   ____
     b. evanescent   b. association
     c. transmittance   c. connubial
     d. transitory   d. conjugal

20. a. asteroid   ____   29. a. nadir   ____
     b. astral   b. apogee
     c. stellar   c. apex
     d. sidereal   d. acme

21. a. fetid   ____   30. a. loquacious   ____
     b. malodorous   b. garrulous
     c. noisome   c. taciturn
     d. clamorous   d. voluble

22. a. melange   ____   31. a. gainsay   ____
     b. homogeneous   b. advocate
     c. potpourri   c. controvert
     d. medley   d. remonstrate

23. a. extraneous   ____   32. a. antipodal   ____
     b. capricious   b. antonym
     c. mercurial   c. analogous
     d. fickle   d. inverse

24. a. pliant   ____   33. a. affable   ____
     b. malleable   b. exacting
     c. refractory   c. stringent
     d. ductile   d. stark

25. a. inconsistent   ____   34. a. aphasia   ____
     b. congruent   b. depletion
     c. discrepant   c. amnesia
     d. incongruous   d. preservation

35. a. nefarious   ____
    b. iniquitous
    c. execrable
    d. dexterous

36. a. sang-froid   ____
    b. consternation
    c. trepidation
    d. apprehension

37. a. affiliated   ____
    b. cognate
    c. antipathy
    d. kindred

38. a. germane   ____
    b. apposite
    c. pertinent
    d. consign

39. a. consequential   ____
    b. picayune
    c. paltry
    d. frivolous

40. a. iniquitous   ____
    b. heinous
    c. exemplary
    d. perverse

41. a. sapient   ____
    b. injudicious
    c. sagacious
    d. politic

42. a. nostrum   ____
    b. emetic
    c. diuretic
    d. toxin

43. a. cliche   ____
    b. unique
    c. trite
    d. platitude

44. a. avowal   ____
    b. recondite
    c. obscure
    d. arcane

45. a. strident   ____
    b. relentless
    c. harmonious
    d. astringent

46. a. noxious   ____
    b. harridan
    c. virulent
    d. malicious

47. a. double entendre   ____
    b. binomial
    c. pas de deux
    d. troika

48. a. rupture   ____
    b. commence
    c. rift
    d. interregnum

49. a. altruistic   ____
    b. eleemosynary
    c. parsimonious
    d. philanthropic

50. a. traverse   ____
    b. recede
    c. stasis
    d. maneuver

51. a. bellicose   ____
    b. pacify
    c. contentious
    d. litigious

52. a. incommodious   ____
    b. exiguous
    c. consequential
    d. iota

53. a. incarcerate
     b. emancipate
     c. exculpate
     d. gratis   ____

54. a. ambiguous
     b. obfuscate
     c. incomprehensible
     d. explicit   ____

55. a. potential
     b. contingent
     c. incredible
     d. eventual   ____

56. a. disaffected
     b. ill-disposed
     c. inimical
     d. amicable   ____

57. a. effete
     b. effective
     c. feckless
     d. tenuous   ____

58. a. dubious
     b. peremptory
     c. categorical
     d. autocratic   ____

59. a. wanton
     b. fulsome
     c. intemperate
     d. deficient   ____

60. a. succinct
     b. diffuse
     c. redundant
     d. prolix   ____

61. a. indefinable
     b. nebulous
     c. explicit
     d. indeterminate   ____

62. a. impeachable
     b. simulate
     c. emulate
     d. parody   ____

63. a. gauche
     b. ungainly
     c. inept
     d. contumacious   ____

64. a. concurrence
     b. dissonance
     c. covenant
     d. consonance   ____

65. a. sine qua non
     b. integral
     c. incidental
     d. inherent   ____

66. a. torpid
     b. imaginative
     c. obtuse
     d. pedestrian   ____

67. a. inauguration
     b. surcease
     c. abort
     d. cloture   ____

68. a. duplicity
     b. scrupulousness
     c. veracity
     d. integrity   ____

69. a. gaunt
     b. jocund
     c. saturnine
     d. somber   ____

70. a. elastic
     b. supple
     c. lissome
     d. intractable   ____

71.   a. pivot   ____
    b. divert
    c. deviate
    d. remain

72.   a. posit   ____
    b. apposite
    c. recommend
    d. propound

73.   a. retire   ____
    b. transcend
    c. levitate
    d. resurgent

74.   a. simulate   ____
    b. feign
    c. simplistic
    d. feint

75.   a. antediluvian   ____
    b. passe
    c. outmoded
    d. chic

76.   a. dolorous   ____
    b. optimistic
    c. lugubrious
    d. plaintive

77.   a. mercurial   ____
    b. vibrant
    c. phlegmatic
    d. piquant

78.   a. insulate   ____
    b. insular
    c. sanctum
    d. combine

79.   a. leotard   ____
    b. sarong
    c. tenacious
    d. vestment

80.   a. contumacious   ____
    b. recalcitrant
    c. compliant
    d. insubordinate

81.   a. exercise   ____
    b. dichotomize
    c. excise
    d. truncate

82.   a. bullock   ____
    b. drake
    c. ram
    d. vixen

83.   a. resume   ____
    b. dissociate
    c. balkanize
    d. disaffiliate

84.   a. factitious   ____
    b. prosthesis
    c. candid
    d. affectation

85.   a. invalidate   ____
    b. enact
    c. abrogate
    d. supersede

86.   a. invoke   ____
    b. convoke
    c. renounce
    d. muster

87.   a. cancel   ____
    b. obliterate
    c. efface
    d. record

88.   a. senile   ____
    b. avant-garde
    c. geriatric
    d. dotage

Angels are able to fly because they take themselves lightly.
—Buddhist Proverb

Be curious always!
For knowledge will not acquire you:
You must acquire it.
—Sudie Back

There's one way to find out if a man is honest — ask him.
If he says, "Yes," you know he's a crook.
—Groucho Marx

The more the marble wastes,
the more the statue grows.
—Michelangelo

He drew a circle that shut me out —
Heretic, rebel, a thing to flout.
But Love and I had the wit to win:
We draw a circle that took him in!
—Edwin Markham

The meaning of life is to give life meaning.
—Ken Hudgins

We should be careful to get out of an experience
only the wisdom that is in it —
and stop there;
lest we be like the cat that sits down on a hot stove lid.
She will never sit down
on a hot stove lid again
—and that is well;
but also she will never sit down on a cold one any more.
—Mark Twain

You may be disappointed if you fail,
but you are doomed, if you don't try.
—Beverly Sills

It often happens that I wake at night and begin to think about
a serious problem and decide I must tell the Pope about it.
Then I wake up completely and remember that I am the Pope!
—Pope John XXIII

Chapter 4: Sentences

Word Comprehension

Select the word or set of words that best complete the meaning of the sentence as a whole. You should use a dictionary to learn the definitions of those words with which you are unfamiliar.

1. Xerxes was __1__ to continue playing by winning a few jackpots.
   a. befitted
   b. controverted
   c. beguiled
   d. exuded

2. Judas was a(n) __1__ liar.
   a. recessive
   b. effete
   c. judicious
   d. egregious

3. Dorothea had one of the __1__ of a good writer, being __2__ at research.
   a. remnants   awkward
   b. indications   detrimental
   c. attributes   adept
   d. symbols   inept

4. A few children forget their __1__ obligations when they grow older.
   a. figurative
   b. prodigious
   c. grandiose
   d. filial

5. We have a(n) __1__ agreement between us.
   a. fervid
   b. inept
   c. tacit
   d. inadvertent

6. Some say the art of politics is seeking a(n) __1__ .
   a. superlative
   b. consensus
   c. abeyance
   d. remuneration

When a man blames others for his failures, it's a good idea to credit
others for his successes. —Howard W. Newton

7. We observed the snake moving in a __1__ manner.
      a. sinuses
      b. synodal   ____
      c. sinistral
      d. sinuous

8. In spite of its limited __1__, the newsletter has a strong __2__ on the
    student body.
      a. merit   perception
      b. appeal   subjugation   ____
      c. dimension   potency
      d. circulation   influence

9. He was aware of the __1__ of his case; nevertheless he remained __2__.
      a. solemnity   grievous
      b. grievousness   robust   ____
      c. gravity   assured
      d. import   malevolent

10. His friends enjoyed his __1__ wit, but his targets often __2__ at its irony.
      a. trenchant   winced
      b. concise   recoiled   ____
      c. tremulous   languished
      d. credulous   aspired

11. Gerald's thesis should be the __1__ work on the subject until new data
    make a revision __2__.
      a. necessary   formative
      b. seminal   essential   ____
      c. unimpassioned   indisputable
      d. halcyon   comprehensible

12. Although her summations are very __1__, her __2__ style often alienates
    the jury.
      a. cogent   bombastic
      b. equivocal   unpretentious   ____
      c. energizing   burly
      d. caustic   assertive

13. Given the current budget crisis, there will be no further __1__ on any
    new programs, at least for the __2__ future.
      a. prospects   peripheral
      b. cynicism   near   ____
      c. expenditures   foreseeable
      d. retrenchment   refutable

82 ©

14. The police studied the suspect's __1__ to discover any __2__ motives.
    a. confession   vicarious   ____
    b. statement   ulterior
    c. home   conscious
    d. record   vanquished

15. Jimmy's __1__ was so obvious that I said he must have seen an __2__.
    a. ruddiness   exhibit   ____
    b. blandness   impression
    c. pallor   apparition
    d. prolixity   embellishment

16. It is __1__ that the best-prepared student should have to resort to __2__ the rules.
    a. ironic   circumventing   ____
    b. implausible   eschewing
    c. incongruous   reconforming
    d. natural   embellishing

17. Letitia's true feelings __1__ themselves in her sarcastic asides; for only then was her __2__ revealed.
    a. obscured   animation   ____
    b. dominated   geniality
    c. agitated   grotesqueness
    d. manifested   cynicism

18. When Ronald realized he had been induced to sign the contract by __1__, he threatened to institute legal proceedings to __2__ the agreement.
    a. chicanery   abrogate   ____
    b. subterfuge   implement
    c. guile   sustain
    d. candor   recant

19. In order to __1__ a sudden outbreak of violence, we must not allow any __2__ to occur.
    a. proffer   proviso   ____
    b. facilitate   affront
    c. preclude   provocation
    d. inhibit   stimulation

20. Since their divorce she __1__ anyone who visits her former husband.
    a. maligns   ____
    b. macerates
    c. countervails
    d. disqualifies

21. World War II was responsible for __1__ new __2__ in the population.

    a. affecting   calumny   ____
    b. obviating   asperity
    c. enlightening   amassment
    d. effecting   aspirations

22. The balloon remained __1__ for awhile and then began to rise __2__.
    a. apparent   rapidly   ____
    b. transfixed   sporadically
    c. stationary   imperceptibly
    d. immutable   insignificantly

23. The dogmatist who __1__ believes in freedom of speech for himself may not for those who __2__ his ideologies.
    a. inherently   repudiate   ____
    b. characteristically countenance
    c. firmly   espouse
    d. superficially   disdain

24. The escaping vapors were highly __1__, yet measures were not taken for the __2__ of the experiment.
    a. noxious   cessation   ____
    b. gaseous   initiating
    c. volatile   disarray
    d. salubrious   respite

25. Every winter tourists __1__ themselves in Arizona and Florida.
    a. resonate   ____
    b. disport
    c. expiate
    d. relegate

26. Since salary increases each year are __1__, his action canceling them was considered __2__.
    a. mendacious   arbitrary   ____
    b. mandatory   capricious
    c. exorbitant   objective
    d. appropriate   arcane

27. The jury was convinced that he was guilty of __1__ since a __2__ of conflicting testimony had been heard.
    a. falsification   superfluity   ____
    b. lying   covenant
    c. perjury   plethora
    d. subornation   vindication

84 ©

28. The Spanish found the potato to be __1__ to South America.
    a. indigent
    b. indeterminate
    c. indigenous
    d. ingenuous

                      ____

29. The United States has agreed to sign a __1__ trade treaty with Canada.
    a. reciprocal
    b. recapitulation
    c. recidivist
    d. recessive

                      ____

30. Chester was widely __1__ for his rhetorical skills and was __2__ for class honors.

a. bequeathed	proposed
b. denounced	acknowledged
c. acclaimed	nominated
d. eulogized	recommended

                      ____

31. Since you disagree with Cicero's arguments in this dispute, your __1__ of his position is __2__.

a. espousal	hypocritical
b. advocacy	feigned
c. furtherance	sincere
d. surmise	deceptive

                      ____

32. My __1__ was __2__ when I heard his explanation.

a. skepticism	reiterated
b. misgiving	dispelled
c. misogyny	startled
d. certainty	aroused

                      ____

33. Counsel attempted to __1__ the jury's impression of his client's guilt by emphasizing Aaron's __2__ character.

a. disenchant	culpable
b. disillusion	iniquitous
c. impair	guileless
d. disabuse	irreproachable

                      ____

34. Large sections in many national parks are being preserved in a(n) __1__ state to remind of us our past.
    a. untamed
    b. unchanged
    c. pristine
    d. pretentious

                      ____

35. His actions are ruled by __1__ rather than ethical considerations.
    a. expediency
    b. morality
    c. idealism
    d. gratification

    ____

36. A(n)__1__ comparison may be a __2__ statement.
    a. frank   true
    b. modest   contrived
    c. ominous   propitious
    d. implied   metaphorical

    ____

37. Caroline does not wish to __1__ your extracurricular activities, but you must __2__ your assignment first.
    a. impute   initiate
    b. constrict   maintain
    c. proscribe   consummate
    d. circumscribe   complete

    ____

38. A(n) __1__ on the manufacture of nuclear weapons may lead to a __2__ treaty.
    a. concession   pacification
    b. moratorium   nonproliferation
    c. indulgence   harmonious
    d. abridgement   conciliatory

    ____

39. Do not be __1__ about your chances since you failed the final examination.
    a. sanguine
    b. portentous
    c. theoretical
    d. assiduous

    ____

40. His rebuttal was __1__; it did not __2__ to the topic.
    a. pertinent   belong
    b. irrelevant   pertain
    c. important   contribute
    d. cogent   relate

    ____

41. The attorney objected to the testimony, saying it was not __1__ to the case.
    a. germane
    b. favorable
    c. salubrious
    d. inimical

    ____

42. The whole scene seemed bright and shiny in the __1__ glow of the early morning sun.
    a. fulsome
    b. fetid
    c. radiant
    d. diaphanous

43. In the interest of fairness, the arbitration board __1__ in the __2__ between the parties.
    a. intruded   disruption
    b. inquired   concession
    c. intercepted   challenge
    d. intervened   dispute

44. The generals were __1__ because their plans had gone __2__.
    a. arrogant   enigmatic
    b. terse   torpid
    c. distraught   awry
    d. testy   moribund

45. If she comes to the meeting with such a(n) __1__ attitude, we will not reach a(n) __2__ agreement.
    a. adamant   mellifluous
    b. obdurate   amicable
    c. inflexible   discordant
    d. amenable   incompatible

46. The congresswoman __1__ her supporters with her __2__ attitude towards the audience.
    a. attracted   extenuating
    b. alienated   truculent
    c. rebuked   proverbial
    d. confounded   celestial

47. The child was not __1__ and preferred to be alone in the school yard.
    a. antisocial
    b. gregarious
    c. sincere
    d. invigorating

48. The junction of the Mississippi and Missouri can be called a __1__.
    a. confinement
    b. confluence
    c. covenant
    d. dissolution

49. Many television programs will use any plot device to __1__ their audiences.
    a. titillate
    b. transmit
    c. personify
    d. renovate

50. The case of Caesar v Brutus was entered in the __1__ for the Ides of March.
    a. prospectus
    b. pendant
    c. abstract
    d. docket

51. A method of remembering a series of items is to use a(n) __1__ device.
    a. mnemonic
    b. rote
    c. ensemble
    d. rhetorical

52. The farmer looked out of place in his __1__ attire.
    a. churlish
    b. deteriorated
    c. grandiloquent
    d. rustic

53. I refuse to accept these statements as __1__.
    a. increments
    b. postulates
    c. moderations
    d. imperiums

54. There was much __1__ as to the __2__ steps needed to reduce the failure rate.
    a. agitation   habitual
    b. criticism   average
    c. deliberation   recurrent
    d. speculation   specific

55. Increased __1__ on textbooks do not necessarily bring results __2__ with the money spent.
    a. receipts   coordinate
    b. expenditures   commensurate
    c. appraisals   consistent
    d. promotions   persistent

56. The Red Cross has attempted to __1__ the conditions of those affected by the hurricane.
    a. ameliorate   ____
    b. bolster
    c. disclaim
    d. invoke

57. The doctor prescribed placebos for Goliath, who is a confirmed __1__.
    a. hyperesthesiac   ____
    b. hypothesiac
    c. hypochondriac
    d. hypercrite

58. Nostradamus read the forecast __1__.
    a. verbose   ____
    b. loquaciously
    c. viably
    d. verbatim

59. The Supreme Court Justices show a(n) __1__ demeanor in public.
    a. frivolous   ____
    b. austere
    c. credible
    d. dissident

60. Despite their seeming __1__, the resistance fighters did their best to __2__ their occupiers.
    a. harmony   assist   ____
    b. assent   abet
    c. acquiescence   thwart
    d. recalcitrance   vindicate

61. Large armies are becoming increasingly __1__, but the military is reluctant to __2__ this fact.
    a. obsolete   concede   ____
    b. powerful   mitigate
    c. enigmatic   enhance
    d. philanthropic   resist

62. She was __1__ to an unimportant job by the new management.
    a. redeemed   ____
    b. expedited
    c. propelled
    d. relegated

Whatever you can do, or dream you can, begin it.
Boldness has genius, power, and magic in it. —Goethe

Recognizing and Correcting Incorrect Sentences

If the following sentences contains an error, enter the letter b and correct the error. If the sentences are correct as is, enter the letter a.

1. If the litmus paper change color to red, an acid is present.
   a. correct   b. incorrect   _____

2. Anyone may watch the trial when they like.
   a. correct   b. incorrect   _____

3. We conducted the experiment under high temperatures also we repeated it at low temperatures.
   a. correct   b. incorrect   _____

4. Crick's and Watson's experiments determined the structure of DNA at the molecular level.
   a. correct   b. incorrect   _____

5. Garret's invention has been replaced by several models of opener (not to mention several kinds of can), each touted to be the best.
   a. correct   b. incorrect   _____

6. I wish I were at the beach today.
   a. correct   b. incorrect   _____

7. My children are three and 6 years old.
   a. correct   b. incorrect   _____

8. After nearly a decade of unfunded research, the back-burner project finally had born thrilling results.
   a. correct   b. incorrect   _____

9. After she acceded to the group's plans, she changed her mind.
   a. correct   b. incorrect   _____

10. She enjoys the opera and ballet, but neither are performed where she lives.
    a. correct   b. incorrect   _____

11. Franklin continues to run 3 miles everyday.
    a. correct   b. incorrect   _____

12. To make matters worse, none of the members of the law firm have much experience in criminal law.
    a. correct   b. incorrect   _____

I'll moider de bum. —Tony Two-Ton Galento

90 ©

13. James had only ones and fives in his wallet.
    a. correct   b. incorrect   ____

14. Would you state your name?
    a. correct   b. incorrect   ____

15. Edith is a conscientious, honest, reliable, worker.
    a. correct   b. incorrect   ____

16. You signed the will; later your wife died.
    a. correct   b. incorrect   ____

17. I wish you would come to the party.
    a. correct   b. incorrect   ____

18. All the rooms have been painted except the mens' room.
    a. correct   b. incorrect   ____

19. What time did you call and ...
    a. correct   b. incorrect   ____

20. Looking West, we saw the Great Plains.
    a. correct   b. incorrect   ____

21. They or Salome are certain to be replace.
    a. correct   b. incorrect   ____

22. Ellen bought a ski rack to carry her skies.
    a. correct   b. incorrect   ____

23. These defense measures were essential to the safety of our nation.
    a. correct   b. incorrect   ____

24. When you looked out the window, what did you see?
    a. correct   b. incorrect   ____

25. The life of a doctor is very busy. They often have to work very long hours.
    a. correct   b. incorrect   ____

26. To who should I sent the transcript?
    a. correct   b. incorrect   ____

27. You too, could have come with us.
    a. correct   b. incorrect   ____

28. Last week we were in court it was in an unheated building.
    a. correct   b. incorrect   ____

29. Her parent's garage was filled with Nona's furniture.
    a. correct   b. incorrect   ____

30. There we were——all of us—John, Mary and me waiting for the trial
    to begin.
    a. correct   b. incorrect   ____

31. You are, obviously, as competent as him.
    a. correct   b. incorrect   ____

32. The principles he lives by interest neither he nor I.
    a. correct   b. incorrect   ____

33. Jim felt bad about the effect of his actions on the others.
    a. correct   b. incorrect   ____

34. First you light the grill and then the meat is grilled.
    a. correct   b. incorrect   ____

35. She is as eligible as or even more eligible than I.
    a. correct   b. incorrect   ____

36. The chances of winning the lottery has not been a serious factor in
    my retirement plans.
    a. correct   b. incorrect   ____

37. The association honored: the dedicated, the devout, and the
    disciplined.
    a. correct   b. incorrect   ____

38. The young man who she wants to marry is a student.
    a. correct   b. incorrect   ____

39. She is confident to be able to complete the transcript by tomorrow.
    a. correct   b. incorrect   ____

40. Between you and me, neither Rufus nor Raquet knows to whom the
    letter should be addressed to.
    a. correct   b. incorrect   ____

41. My lawyer agreed to council Canute about his administrative duties.
    a. correct   b. incorrect   ____

42. Our PBS station asked for 30, 40, or 50 dollars as a yearly pledge.
    a. correct   b. incorrect   ____

43. Did you wish your laboratory partner to be he?
    a. correct   b. incorrect   ____

44. It was a act that caused consternation to all his friends.
    a. correct   b. incorrect   ____

45. George's grades are as good as if not better then Florence's.
    a. correct   b. incorrect   ____

46. My student Grace, has completed her thesis.
    a. correct   b. incorrect   ____

47. As he ascended the mountain Garret slipped and plunges hundreds of feet to his death.
    a. correct   b. incorrect   ____

48. Barbara writes very well but has difficulty expressing her ideas verbally.
    a. correct   b. incorrect   ____

49. Draco goes to every meeting of the senate of course.
    a. correct   b. incorrect   ____

50. Nero bought nine dollars worth of violin strings.
    a. correct   b. incorrect   ____

51. The courthouse is near to the town square.
    a. correct   b. incorrect   ____

52. My lawyer did not give me very good advise.
    a. correct   b. incorrect   ____

53. He wants neither fame or fortune.
    a. correct   b. incorrect   ____

54. The letter said not to do any changes until I heard from you.
    a. correct   b. incorrect   ____

55. They can do whatever they chose.
    a. correct   b. incorrect   ____

Alas, I know if I ever became truly humble, I would be proud of it.
—Benjamin Franklin

56. The director plans to alternate the role between Huey, Louie, and Dewey.
    a. correct   b. incorrect   ____

57. Everyone has a favorite anecdote they tell their friends.
    a. correct   b. incorrect   ____

58. Statistics can be cited to prove that prices this year are lower than last year.
    a. correct   b. incorrect   ____

59. The explosion was too loud for me not to hear.
    a. correct   b. incorrect   ____

60. The lawyer asked, "When were you hired at Dudley Dorite Inc.?"
    a. correct   b. incorrect   ____

61. Wear and tear have to be expected when you buy a used item.
    a. correct   b. incorrect   ____

62. No thanks is due to you for this.
    a. correct   b. incorrect   ____

63. The judge fined Henry and she for contempt.
    a. correct   b. incorrect   ____

64. Red Ridinghood has not called nor written since she left home.
    a. correct   b. incorrect   ____

65. We know that our animal was the most unique cat in the show.
    a. correct   b. incorrect   ____

66. Theodora had not been in the office but a few minutes when she became sick.
    a. correct   b. incorrect   ____

67. Of the five three passed the examination.
    a. correct   b. incorrect   ____

68. The witness said that, "I was not there."
    a. correct   b. incorrect   ____

69. "Why did you leave the building", his lawyer asked.
    a. correct   b. incorrect   ____

70. When you used the phrase "too fast," what did you mean?
    a. correct   b. incorrect   ____

71. Whom you know is very important in politics.
    a. correct   b. incorrect   ____

72. Our supervisor selected Homer and myself to go.
    a. correct   b. incorrect   ____

73. The counselor thought she could help Claudia's family, but the other's problems were too complicated.
    a. correct   b. incorrect   ____

74. "I began college in 1992," she said. "I plan to complete my courses in three years".
    a. correct   b. incorrect   ____

75. Grace came to school in the morning, and prepared her speech in the library.
    a. correct   b. incorrect   ____

76. The referee understood the situation immediately he must give the player a penalty shot.
    a. correct   b. incorrect   ____

77. Walter moved to the west sometime during the 1980s.
    a. correct   b. incorrect   ____

78. Let me ask mother if I can stay late that night.
    a. correct   b. incorrect   ____

79. Snow, severe cold, wind—these best describe our last winter storm.
    a. correct   b. incorrect   ____

80. What recourse does Student A. have if Professor X. does not return her term paper?
    a. correct   b. incorrect   ____

81. Any Senator may offer a bill during the legislative session.
    a. correct   b. incorrect   ____

82. He always brings both a pen and pencil.
    a. correct   b. incorrect   ____

83. 1992 was not a good year for our stockholders.
    a. correct   b. incorrect   ____

84. Ishmael came football practice, but did not partake in any drills.
    a. correct   b. incorrect   ____

85. The teacher told the class there would be no ifs, ands, or buts regarding late assignments.
    a. correct   b. incorrect   ____

86. Eleanor said, "I heard Franklin telephone Anna and ask, `will you go to the opera with us'?"
    a. correct   b. incorrect   ____

87. During the last few years, defense spending has been reduced.
    a. correct   b. incorrect   ____

88. The State of Arizona entered the Union in 1912 as the forty-eighth state.
    a. correct   b. incorrect   ____

89. My motel room during the conference cost $75: hers $80, Adlai's $90.
    a. correct   b. incorrect   ____

90. He said, "it wont happen again."
    a. correct   b. incorrect   ____

91. The job application required (a) name, (b) address, (c) previous employers, and (d) references.
    a. correct   b. incorrect   ____

92. He was considered to be a garrulous, friendly, popular, teacher.
    a. correct   b. incorrect   ____

93. The committee wanted to know when he knew it, how much he knew, and why he did not report the incident?
    a. correct   b. incorrect   ____

94. "Semiannual" does not have the same meaning as "biennial."
    a. correct   b. incorrect   ____

95. She learned her three R's and brought home a report card with two A's and three B's.
    a. correct   b. incorrect   ____

96. If I was to win the lottery, I wouldn't have to work anymore.
    a. correct   b. incorrect   ____

97. Are you the owner of Arbor-Lawn Inc.?
    a. correct   b. incorrect   ____

98. Several agencies refused to fund us: the project was considered too avant garde.
    a. correct   b. incorrect   ____

99. As a playwrite, three-quarters of his talent lies in the dialogues he writes.
    a. correct   b. incorrect   ____

100. The Senator from Texas voted against the bill.
    a. correct   b. incorrect   ____

101. We were the two last players to be selected in the football draft.
    a. correct   b. incorrect   ____

102. Not only were you speeding, also your brakes were defective.
    a. correct   b. incorrect   ____

103. I will speak to whomever is there.
    a. correct   b. incorrect   ____

104. Her mother objected to Colette playing her radio loudly.
    a. correct   b. incorrect   ____

105. Nefertiti disagreed with the project as outlined by Tutankhamen.
    a. correct   b. incorrect   ____

106. Everyone attended the meeting but I.
    a. correct   b. incorrect   ____

The bumper's only use is as a Braille device to help you park.
—Eugene Bordinat

You know, I'm starting to wonder what my folks were up to
at my age that makes them so suspicious of me all the time.
—Margaret Blair

One loyal friend is worth ten thousand relatives.
—Unknown Author

A doctor can busy his mistakes, but an architect
can only advise his clients to plant vines. —Frank Loyd Wright

The earth does not belong to man:
Man belongs to the earth.
This we know: All things are connected.
Like the blood which unites one family.
All things are connected.
Whatever befalls the earth Befalls the sons of the earth.
Man did not weave the web of life.
He is merely a strand in it.
Whatever he does to the web,
He does to himself.
—Chief Seattle

Talk does not cook rice. —Chinese Proverb

A dog is a dog except when he's facing you. Then he is Mr. Dog.
—Unknown Haitian Farmer

You arx a kxy pxrson. Xvxn
though my typxwritxr is an old modxl,
it works vxry wxll — xxcxpt for onx kxy.
You would think that with all thx othxr kxys
functioning propxrly, onx kxy not working
would hardly bx noticxd.
But just onx kxy out of whack
sxxms to ruin thx wholx xffort.
You may say to yoursxlf,
"Wxll, I'm only onx pxrson. No onx
will noticx if I don't do my bxst."
But it doxs makx a diffxrxncs, bxcausx to
bx xffxctivx, an organization nxxds activx
participation by xvxronx to thx bxst of his
or hxr ability.
So thx nxxt timx you think you arx
not important, rxmxmbxr my old typxwritxer.
You arx a kxy pxrson.
—Author Unknown

I don't do anything that's bad for me.
I don't like to be made nervous or angry.
Anytime you get upset it tears down your nervous system.
—Mae West

I believe my theory of relativity to be true.
But it will only be proved for certain in 1981, when I am dead.
—Albert Einstein, 1938 (1879 - 1955)

****Pedagogically sound covering a wealth of material
with facts, tips, information.   Time-Tested, Proven
In the Classroom and Independent Study****

The world's largest library of *court reporter training, *private tutoring, *career coaching, *test prep!

Complete NCRA and State RPR, RDR, CSR WKT Test Prep Textbook, 6th Edition, Updated/Revised

<u>2015 Sixth Edition</u> *Textbook*: Only textbook on the market! Latin, legal, court terms; detailed grammar, punctuation; vocabulary; medical; Expanded **Test-Taking Tips; **Additional Focus Tips; ** Updated/Expanded Computer Terminology, **Technology, **Advisory Opinions, **Ethics

Workbook follows the *Complete WKT Text*: <u>testing resource</u> with Latin, legal, court terms; grammar; vocabulary; medical; computer sections -- <u>approximately 2,002 practice test questions</u>

Companion Workbook Study Guide follows the *Workbook*, cross-referencing each word, showing where and how words are used. Learn why an answer is correct, incorrect, or the distracting answer

** "Test Prep Set" – four-volume set – is CRRbooks.com's bestseller consisting of the *Complete WKT Textbook, Workbook, Companion Study Guide,* and *Realtime Vocabulary Workbook* **

Vastly improve skills for greater career opportunities with CART Captioning and court reporting.

*Learn *How* to Test. ** Pass the first time!

Join the thousands of students, novice and long-time professionals who have discovered:
- The highest-result NCRA and State Test Prep Textbook and Workbooks for testing success;
- Affordable tutoring and confidential one-on-one private coaching for your accelerated progress;
- Simple time-management and organized motivational skills to keep you moving forward.

*Are you struggling with tests, motivation, personal challenges, focus, and/or speedbuilding?

Veteran court reporter, Monette Benoit, multiple-title author of books and test prep for the CART Captioning and reporting industry helps clients achieve at higher levels. Build new strengths in testing, focus, and speedbuilding. **Email <u>Monette@CRRbooks.com</u> about <u>tutoring</u>, <u>coaching packages</u>.**

Nationally known as the *Court Reporting Whisperer*, Monette provides tutoring and career coaching.

Get the latest tips and advice from **www.monettebenoit.com** and **www.CRRbooks.com**
"Monette's Musings" contains information for busy professionals and students.

**NEW: RealTime Dictionary Builder, <u>www.realtimedictionarybuilder.com</u>
Championed by Kathy DiSanti DiLorenzo, RDR-CRR-CBC, and many others.**

As a student, I felt inclined to study this material as I did academic tests. Much of the material reviewed appeared on the exam. **This text is a wonderful tool** that should be utilized by students and reporters everywhere as an aid in passing written tests. **– Laura Ballard, RPR, CSR – Ex-Student**

Having been a captioner and out of reporting and testing arenas, I knew I would cram for the NCRA RDR, Registered Diplomate Reporter, exam. I chose **this textbook** and the <u>REALTIME Vocabulary Workbook</u> to bring myself up to date – and how out of date I was! **These books have excellent study material for the CSR, RPR, and RMR.** I received my RDR results. Thanks, Monette! **– Kathy DiSanti DiLorenzo, *RDR-CRR-CBC***

To join our successful ranks, go to: www.CRRbooks.com

Roots, Prefixes, Suffixes
Page 1

Section 1
a. 9
b. 7
c. 5
d. 10
e. 2
f. 1
g. 4
h. 3
i. 8
j. 6

Section 2
a. 18
b. 15
c. 20
d. 11
e. 17
f. 12
g. 19
h. 14
i. 16
j. 13

Section 3
a. 24
b. 28
c. 30
d. 21
e. 27
f. 22
g. 29
h. 23
i. 26
j. 25

Section 4
a. 38
b. 34
c. 40

d. 31
e. 37
f. 33
g. 39
h. 35
i. 32
j. 36

Section 5
a. 50
b. 46
c. 44
d. 48
e. 41
f. 49
g. 42
h. 43
i. 47
j. 45

Section 6
a. 56
b. 60
c. 51
d, 58
e. 52
f. 59
g. 54
h. 57
i. 53
j. 55

Section 7
a. 67
b. 70
c. 61
d. 68
e. 62
f. 69
g. 64
h. 66
i. 63
j. 65

Section 8
a. 73
b. 78
c. 71
d. 80
e. 72
f. 79
g. 74
h. 76
i. 75
j. 77

Section 9
a. 84
b. 90
c. 87
d. 82
e. 89
f. 81
g. 88
h. 85
i. 86
j. 83

Section 10
a. 96
b. 98
c. 91
d. 100
e. 92
f. 99
g. 94
h. 93
i. 97
j. 95

Section 11
a. 106
b. 110
c. 104
d. 108
e. 109
f. 103
g. 101

h. 105
i. 102
j. 107

Section 12
a. 116
b. 120
c. 117
d. 111
e. 119
f. 115
g. 112
h. 114
i. 113
j. 118

Similar Suffixes
Page 5

Section 1
a. 7
b. 4
c. 9
d. 1
e. 10
f. 3
g. 8
h. 5
i. 2
j. 6

Section 2
a. 14
b. 18
c. 11
d. 17
e. 13
f. 20
g. 15
h. 16
i. 19
j. 12

100 ©

Section 3
a.   27
b.   24
c.   30
d.   26
e.   21
f.   28
g.   23
h.   25
i.   22
j.   29

Section 4
a.   40
b.   37
c.   35
d.   38
e.   32
f.   39
g.   34
h.   33
i.   36
j.   31

Section 5
a.   46
b.   50
c.   48
d.   41
e.   49
f.   43
g.   42
h.   45
i.   47
j.   44

Section 6
a.   53
b.   57
c.   55
d.   60
e.   58
f.   51
g.   59

h.   52
i.   56
j.   54

Section 7
a.   67
b.   65
c.   68
d.   70
e.   69
f.   64
g.   63
h.   62
i.   61
j.   66

Section 8
a.   76
b.   73
c.   78
d.   77
e.   80
f.   79
g.   71
h.   75
i.   72
j.   74

Section 9
a.   87
b.   85
c.   88
d.   90
e.   81
f.   89
g.   82
h.   84
i.   86
j.   83

Section 10
a.   95
b.   94
c.   97

d.   99
e.   92
f.   98
g.   93
h.   100
i.   91
j.   96

Section 11
a.   104
b.   109
c.   106
d.   108
e.   103
f.   110
g.   102
h.   107
i.   105
j.   101

Section 12
a.   115
b.   117
c.   113
d.   118
e.   111
f.   120
g.   114
h.   112
i.   116
j.   119

Section 13
a.   129
b.   126
c.   128
d.   122
e.   130
f.   124
g.   125
h.   121
i.   127
j.   123

Section 14
a.   133
b.   137
c.   140
d.   139
e.   136
f.   138
g.   134
h.   131
i.   135
j.   132

Foreign Words
and Phrases
Page 11

Section 1
a.   8
b.   5
c.   10
d.   1
e.   3
f.   9
g.   2
h.   6
i.   4
j.   7

Section 2
a.   14
b.   17
c.   20
d.   12
e.   18
f.   11
g.   19
h.   16
i.   13
j.   15

Section 3
a.   30
b.   25
c.   28

d.	29	Section 7		h.	95	Section 2	
e.	27	a.	69	i.	98	a.	18
f.	24	b.	67	j.	92	b.	14
g.	22	c.	70			c.	16
h.	23	d.	66	Section 11		d.	12
i.	21	e.	62	a.	106	e.	20
j.	26	f.	64	b.	109	f.	11
		g.	63	c.	105	g.	19
Section 4		h.	65	d.	108	h.	13
a.	40	i.	61	e.	107	i.	15
b.	36	j.	68	f.	104	j.	17
c.	31			g.	103		
d.	38	Section 8		h.	102	Section 3	
e.	33	a.	78	i.	110	a.	30
f.	39	b.	80	j.	101	b.	28
g.	34	c.	76			c.	29
h.	32	d.	71	Section 12		d.	27
i.	37	e.	77	a.	115	e.	24
j.	35	f.	72	b.	117	f.	22
		g.	75	c.	111	g.	25
Section 5		h.	79	d.	118	h.	26
a.	47	i.	74	e.	120	i.	23
b.	45	j.	73	f.	112	j.	21
c.	49			g.	119		
d.	42	Section 9		h.	113	Section 4	
e.	48	a.	88	i.	116	a.	40
f.	41	b.	90	j.	114	b.	37
g.	44	c.	87			c.	39
h.	50	d.	85	Confusing Words		d.	36
i.	46	e.	81	Matching Columns		e.	38
j.	43	f.	89	Page 15		f.	33
		g.	84			g.	35
Section 6		h.	82	Section 1		h.	32
a.	60	i.	86	a.	10	i.	34
b.	56	j.	83	b.	6	j.	31
c.	51			c.	1		
d.	58	Section 10		d.	8	Section 5	
e.	53	a.	97	e.	3	a.	46
f.	59	b.	93	f.	9	b.	50
g.	52	c.	100	g.	2	c.	48
h.	54	d.	91	h.	4	d.	47
i.	57	e.	99	i.	7	e.	42
j.	55	f.	94	j.	5	f.	49
		g.	96			g.	44

h. 43
i. 41
j. 45

Section 6
a. 57
b. 60
c. 58
d. 59
e. 56
f. 52
g. 51
h. 54
i. 55
j. 53

Section 7
a. 70
b. 66
c. 69
d. 67
e. 68
f. 63
g. 65
h. 61
i. 64
j. 62

Section 8
a. 80
b. 77
c. 75
d. 79
e. 78
f. 72
g. 73
h. 71
i. 74
j. 76

Similar Word Columns
Page 18

Section 1
a. 13
b. 3
c. 19
d. 9
e. 20
f. 17
g. 1
h. 15
i. 5
j. 11
k. 14
l. 4
m. 6
n. 16
o. 7
p. 18
q. 2
r. 10
s. 12
t. 8

Section 2
a. 25
b. 31
c. 29
d. 39
e. 36
f. 21
g. 37
h. 27
i. 34
j. 24
k. 35
l. 40
m. 26
n. 30
o. 32
p. 22
q. 38

r. 28
s. 33
t. 23

Eponym Columns
Page 19

Section 1
a. 8
b. 4
c. 9
d. 1
e. 7
f. 3
g. 10
h. 6
i. 2
j. 5

Section 2
a. 15
b. 20
c. 11
d. 16
e. 13
f. 19
g. 12
h. 14
i. 17
j. 18

Section 3
a. 30
b. 26
c. 21
d. 27
e. 22
f. 29
g. 24
h. 25
i. 23
j. 28

Section 4
a. 37
b. 34
c. 38
d. 40
e. 32
f. 31
g. 39
h. 36
i. 35
j. 33

Eponym Definitions
Page 21
1. a
2. c
3. b
4. c
5. d
6. b
7. d
8. a
9. c
10. b
11. b
12. a
13. d
14. b
15. c
16. a
17. d
18. b
19. c
20. b
21. a
22. d
23. b
24. d
25. d

Hyphenation Columns
Page 25   Source: Paragon House Spelling Dictionary, 1993.

Section 1
1. na-palm
2. rac-on-teur
3. amaze
4. shouldn't
5. C
6. tit-il-late
7. C
8. C
9. magi-cal
10. C

Section 2
11. im-pera-tive
12. ubi-ety
13. sell-ers
14. C
15. rhythm
16. brac-er
17. C
18. in-ter-ro-gate
19. over-ac-tive
20. C

Section 3
21. chil-dren
22. re-fer-al
23. pa-raly-sis
24. C
25. codi-cil
26. pe-rim-eter
27. C
28. gal-axy
29. minia-ture
30. machine-gun

Section 4
31. C
32. in-ter-rogative
33. va-lid-ity
34. C
35. C
36. into
37. C
38. C
39. undo
40. stat-is-ti-cian

Section 5
41. for-mal-ize
42. an-ec-do-tal
43. thera-pist
44. C
45. C
46. fidg-et
47. C
48. vacuum
49. bi-sym-met-ry
50. ame-nable

Section 6
51. C
52. bis-tro
53. xen-on
54. C
55. anal-ogy
56. va-ri-etal
57. cat-egori-cal
58. C
59. C
60. unani-mous

Section 7
61. C
62. theo-logi-cal
63. hetero-doxy
64. C

65. re-ferred
66. para-lyze
67. C
68. feud
69. ma-caw
70. C

Section 8
71. C
72. psycho-gen-esis
73. C
74. carou-sel
75. urol-ogy
76. ex-on-era-tion
77. hell-ish
78. syba-rite
79. depu-tize
80. C

Section 9
81. C
82. kin-dred-ship
83. C
84. fibu-la
85. ge-nealo-gist
86. zoo-logi-cal
87. ca-rot-id
88. de-spond-ent
89. C
90. exo-dus

Section 10
91. kin-der-gar-ten
92. ma-laise
93. C
94. par-ox-ysm
95. frui-tion
96. Xer-ox
97. C
98. liga-ture
99. C
100. C

Section 11
101. ico-nog-ra-phy
102. pa-rol
103. C
104. C
105. C
106. natu-ral-is-tic
107. quali-fy
108. se-rial-ly
109. jump-off
110. C

Section 12
111. C
112. C
113. radio-graph-ic
114. oblig-ing
115. mana-gerial
116. top-ic
117. ra-di-olo-gist
118. neg-li-gent
119. iso-mer
120. me-dici-nal

Misspelled Words
Page 27
1. c
2. a
3. b
4. a
5. d
6. d
7. a
8. c
9. a
10. d
11. c
12. b
13. a
14. b
15. b

16.	c	60.	d	14.	b	58.	a
17.	a	61.	a	15.	b	59.	a
18.	d	62.	a	16.	a	60.	a
19.	a	63.	c	17.	a	61.	b
20.	b	64.	c	18.	b	62.	b
21.	d	65.	b	19.	a	63.	a
22.	d	66.	d	20.	b	64.	a
23.	c	67.	b	21.	b	65.	b
24.	a	68.	c	22.	a	66.	a
25.	b	69.	b	23.	b	67.	a
26.	c	70.	a	24.	a	68.	b
27.	a	71.	c	25.	a	69.	b
28.	d	72.	d	26.	b	70.	b
29.	a	73.	b	27.	a	71.	a
30.	a	74.	d	28.	b	72.	a
31.	c	75.	d	29.	b	73.	b
32.	b	76.	b	30.	a	74.	a
33.	c	77.	a	31.	a	75.	b
34.	a	78.	d	32.	a	76.	b
35.	d	79.	a	33.	b	77.	a
36.	c	80.	d	34.	a	78.	a
37.	d	81.	c	35.	b	79.	b
38.	a	82.	d	36.	a	80.	b
39.	a	83.	c	37.	a	81.	a
40.	a	84.	a	38.	b	82.	b
41.	b	85.	b	39.	a	83.	a
42.	c	86.	c	40.	b	84.	b
43.	a			41.	a	85.	a
44.	d	Misspelled Word		42.	b	86.	a
45.	c	Columns		43.	b	87.	b
46.	c	Page 32		44.	a	88.	a
47.	b	1.	b	45.	a	89.	b
48.	a	2.	a	46.	b	90.	b
49.	a	3.	a	47.	a	91.	a
50	c	4.	a	48.	b	92.	a
51.	b	5.	a	49.	a	93.	b
52.	d	6.	b	50	b	94.	a
53.	c	7.	a	51.	b	95.	a
54.	a	8.	b	52.	a	96.	a
55.	c	9.	b	53.	a	97.	b
56.	d	10.	a	54.	b	98.	a
57.	d	11.	a	55.	a	99.	a
58.	a	12.	b	56.	a	100.	b
59.	c	13.	a	57.	b	101.	a

102.	b	22.	b	**Misspelled Plural**		d.	9
103.	a	23.	a	**Words**		e.	1
104.	b	24.	c	Page 39		f.	5
105.	a	25.	d	1.	d	g.	4
106.	a	26.	a	2.	b	h.	3
107.	b	27.	c	3.	a	i.	7
108.	b	28.	c	4.	a	j.	2
109.	a	29.	a	5.	c		
110.	b	30.	d	6.	d	**Section 2**	
111.	a	31.	b	7.	a	a.	15
112.	b	32.	d	8.	b	b.	20
113.	b	33.	b	9.	d	c.	18
114.	b	34.	b	10.	c	d.	16
115.	a	35.	a	11.	b	e.	11
116.	a	36.	c	12.	a	f.	19
117.	b	37.	c	13.	c	g.	13
118.	b	38.	c	14.	b	h.	14
119.	a	39.	c	15.	a	i.	17
120.	b	40.	d	16.	c	j.	12
		41.	a	17.	b		
Misspelled		42.	b	18.	c	**Section 3**	
Compound Words		43.	a	19.	a	a.	28
Page 35		44.	a	20.	c	b.	30
1.	a	45.	b	21.	d	c.	27
2.	b	46.	d	22.	c	d.	26
3.	d	47.	a	23.	d	e.	29
4.	b	48.	a	24.	a	f.	22
5.	c	49.	b	25.	b	g.	24
6.	c	50.	a	26.	d	h.	21
7.	d	51.	c	27.	d	i.	25
8.	a	52.	b	28.	b	j.	23
9.	d	53.	d	29.	c		
10.	a	54.	a	30.	c	**Section 4**	
11.	a	55.	b	31.	d	a.	39
12.	d	56.	a	32.	c	b.	36
13.	b	57.	c	33.	a	c.	40
14.	a	58.	c			d.	35
15.	c	59.	d	**Abbreviations**		e.	37
16.	a	60.	c	Page 41		f.	32
17.	c	61.	a			g.	38
18.	b	62.	d	**Section 1**		h.	33
19.	a	63.	d	a.	10	i.	31
20.	c	64.	a	b.	8	j.	34
21.	a			c.	6		

Section 5

a.	44
b.	48
c.	46
d.	50
e.	42
f.	47
g.	49
h.	45
i.	41
j.	43

Section 6

a.	55
b.	59
c.	57
d.	51
e.	58
f.	53
g.	60
h.	56
i.	52
j.	54

Compound Words
Page 43

1.	b, c
2.	b, c
3.	b
4.	a
5.	b, c
6.	a, c
7.	a
8.	b
9.	a, c, e
10.	b
11.	a, d
12.	b, d
13.	a, d
14.	a, d
15.	b, c
16.	b, c
17.	a
18.	a, c, e, h

19.	a, d
20.	b, c
21.	b, c, e, g
22.	a, d
23.	a, d, e
24.	a, c, e, h
25.	a, c
26.	b
27.	b, d
28.	b, c, f
29.	a, c, e, h
30.	b
31.	a
32.	a, c, e
33.	a, c, f, g
34.	b, c
35.	b, d, f
36.	b
37.	a, d, f
38.	a, c, e
39.	b, d

Pairs of Spelling
Errors
Page 47

1.	a, c
2.	b, c
3.	c, d
4.	a, b
5.	c, d
6.	a, c
7.	b, d
8.	a, b
9.	a, d
10.	b, d
11.	a, c
12.	a, b
13.	b, c
14.	a, c
15.	b, d
16.	a, d
17.	b, c
18.	a, c
19.	b, c

20.	b, d
21.	b, c
22.	a, c
23.	b, d
24.	a, c
25.	a, d
26.	b, c
27.	b, d
28.	a, d
29.	c, d
30.	a, c
31.	c, d
32.	a, c
33.	a, d
34.	a, c
35.	a, d
36.	b, c
37.	a, d
38.	c, d
39.	a, d
40.	b, c
41.	a, c
42.	b, d
43.	b, d
44.	a, b
45.	b, c
46.	a, b
47.	a, c
48.	b, c
49.	c, d
50.	c, d
51.	a, b
52.	a, c
53.	a, b
54.	b, c
55.	b, d
56.	a, c
57.	a, b
58.	b, c
59.	a, c
60.	b, d
61.	a, d
62.	a, c
63.	b, c

64.	b, d
65.	c, d
66.	b, d

Synonym Matching
Columns
Page 51

Section 1

a.	8
b.	3
c.	7
d.	1
e.	9
f.	5
g.	10
h.	4
i.	6
j.	2

Section 2

a.	17
b.	14
c.	11
d.	19
e.	16
f.	12
g.	18
h.	20
i.	15
j.	13

Section 3

a.	24
b.	26
c.	30
d.	27
e.	21
f.	28
g.	22
h.	29
i.	25
j.	23

Section 4
a. 39
b. 35
c. 37
d. 40
e. 38
f. 32
g. 34
h. 36
i. 33
j. 31

Section 5
a. 44
b. 47
c. 49
d. 41
e. 50
f. 43
g. 48
h. 46
i. 42
j. 45

Section 6
a. 60
b. 55
c. 57
d. 51
e. 56
f. 53
g. 59
h. 52
i. 54
j. 58

Section 7
a. 67
b. 63
c. 65
d. 61
e. 70
f. 68
g. 64

h. 69
i. 62
j. 66

Section 8
a. 75
b. 73
c. 78
d. 71
e. 80
f. 72
g. 79
h. 74
i. 77
j. 76

Section 9
a. 83
b. 85
c. 81
d. 88
e. 87
f. 89
g. 82
h. 90
i. 86
j. 84

Section 10
a. 99
b. 97
c. 100
d. 91
e. 93
f. 98
g. 92
h. 95
i. 94
j. 96

Section 11
a. 10
b. 110
c. 101

d. 107
e. 108
f. 102
g. 105
h. 109
i. 104
j. 106

Section 12
a. 120
b. 116
c. 118
d. 115
e. 119
f. 114
g. 112
h. 113
i. 111
j. 117

Section 13
a. 129
b. 125
c. 130
d. 126
e. 127
f. 128
g. 122
h. 124
i. 123
j. 121

Section 14
a. 138
b. 137
c. 140
d. 131
e. 139
f. 132
g. 134
h. 136
i. 135
j. 133

Antonym Matching Columns
Page 56

Section 1
a. 10
b. 8
c. 4
d. 9
e. 6
f. 1
g. 5
h. 3
i. 2
j. 7

Section 2
a. 13
b. 19
c. 17
d. 20
e. 18
f. 11
g. 15
h. 12
i. 16
j. 14

Section 3
a. 28
b. 26
c. 30
d. 27
e. 23
f. 29
g. 22
h. 24
i. 25
j. 21

108 ©

12.	c	23.	b, d	16.	d, S
13.	a	24.	c, d	17.	b, A
14.	c	25.	a, d	18.	c, A
15.	d	26.	a, d	19.	a, A
16.	c	27.	b, d	20.	b, A
17.	a	28.	c, d	21.	b, S
18.	d	29.	a, c	22.	a, A
19.	b	30.	a, d	23.	d, S

Synonym Sentences

Page 57

1. b
2. d
3. a
4. a
5. b
6. c
7. b
8. d
9. b
10. a
11. d
12. d
13. a
14. c
15. a
16. d
17. b
18. c
19. d
20. b

Selecting Antonyms

Page 60

1. b
2. b
3. c
4. d
5. a
6. d
7. a
8. a
9. c
10. b
11. a

20. b
21. c
22. c
23. d
24. d
25. c
26. b
27. d
28. c
29. a
30. d

Antonyms

Page 62

1. a, b
2. a, c
3. c, d
4. b, d
5. a, c
6. a, d
7. a, d
8. b, c
9. b, c
10. a, d
11. b, d
12. a, c
13. a, c
14. b, c
15. a, c
16. a, d
17. b, d
18. c, d
19. c, d
20. b, d
21. a, b
22. a, c

31. a, b
32. c, d
33. b, c
34. a, c
35. b, d
36. a, c
37. a, b
38. b, d
39. a, d
40. b, c
41. b, c
42. c, d
43. a, b
44. c, d
45. a, c
46. b, d

Synonyms and Antonyms Using Analogy

Page 65

1. c, S
2. b, A
3. d, S
4. a, A
5. b, S
6. c, S
7. a, S
8. d, A
9. c, S
10. a, S
11. b, A
12. d, A
13. c, S
14. b, A
15. a, S

24. c, A
25. b, S
26. a, A
27. c, S
28. a, S
29. d, S
30. b, S
31. c, A
32. d, A
33. a, A
34. c, S
35. a, A
36. d, A
37. b, S
38. b, S
39. a, S
40. b, A
41. c, A
42. d, A
43. b, S
44. a, S
45. c, A
46. b, A
47. d, A
48. a, A
49. b, S
50 a, A
51. d, S
52. b, A
53. a, S
54. c, S
55. b, S
56. c, A
57. b, A
58. a, S
59. d, A

60.	a, S	34.	c, A	25.	b	69.	b
61.	d, S	35.	a, S	26.	d	70.	d
62.	a, A	36.	a, S	27.	b	71.	d
63.	c, S	37.	c, S	28.	b	72.	b
64.	a, A	38.	a, S	29.	a	73.	a
65.	d, S	39.	d, A	30.	c	74.	c
66.	c, S	40.	a, A	31.	b	75.	d
		41.	b, A	32.	c	76.	b

Select Antonym or Synonym
Page 71

42.	d, A	33.	a	77.	c
43.	c, S	34.	d	78.	d
44.	b, S	35.	d	79.	c
1.	b, S	45.	a, S	36.	a	80.	c
2.	c, S	46.	c, A	37.	c	81.	a
3.	d, A	47.	d, S	38.	d	82.	d
4.	b, A	48.	b, A	39.	a	83.	a
5.	c, A	49.	c, A	40.	c	84.	c
6.	a, A	50	c, S	41.	b	85.	b
7.	c, S			42.	d	86.	c
8.	c, A	**Unrelated Words**		43.	b	87.	d
9.	b, A	Page 75		44.	a	88.	b
10.	d, S	1.	a	45.	c		
11.	c, S	2.	d	46.	b	**Word Comprehension**	
12.	c, S	3.	b	47.	d	Page 80	
13.	b, S	4.	a	48.	b		
14.	d, S	5.	c	49.	c	1.	c
15.	c, A	6.	d	50	c	2.	d
16.	a, S	7.	b	51.	b	3.	c
17.	c, A	8.	c	52.	c	4.	d
18.	b, A	9.	c	53.	a	5.	c
19.	d, S	10.	b	54.	d	6.	b
20.	a, S	11.	a	55.	c	7.	d
21.	d, S	12.	d	56.	d	8.	d
22.	b, A	13.	b	57.	b	9.	c
23.	c, S	14.	c	58.	a	10.	a
24.	a, S	15.	a	59.	d	11.	b
25.	b, A	16.	c	60.	a	12.	a
26.	d, S	17.	a	61.	c	13.	c
27.	b, A	18.	d	62.	a	14.	b
28.	b, A	19.	c	63.	d	15.	c
29.	d, A	20.	a	64.	b	16.	a
30.	b, S	21.	d	65.	c	17.	d
31.	d, A	22.	b	66.	b	18.	a
32.	c, A	23.	a	67.	a	19.	c
33.	b, A	24.	c	68.	a	20.	a

21.	d		Incorrect Sentences		43.	b		87.	a
22.	c		Page 89		44.	b		88.	b
23.	a		1.	b	45.	b		89.	b
24.	a		2.	b	46.	b		90.	b
25.	b		3.	b	47.	b		91.	a
26.	b		4.	b	48.	b		92.	b
27.	c		5.	a	49.	b		93.	b
28.	c		6.	a	50	b		94.	a
29.	a		7.	b	51.	b		95.	a
30.	c		8.	b	52.	b		96.	b
31.	a		9.	a	53.	b		97.	a
32.	b		10.	b	54.	b		98.	b
33.	d		11.	a	55.	b		99.	b
34.	c		12.	b	56.	b		100.	a
35.	a		13.	a	57.	b		101.	b
36.	d		14.	b	58.	b		102.	b
37.	d		15.	b	59.	a		103.	b
38.	b		16.	a	60.	a		104.	b
39.	a		17.	a	61.	b		105.	b
40.	b		18.	b	62.	b		106.	b
41.	a		19.	a	63.	b			
42.	c		20.	b	64.	b			
43.	d		21.	b	65.	b			
44.	c		22.	b	66.	b			
45.	b		23.	b	67.	b			
46.	b		24.	a	68.	b			
47.	b		25.	b	69.	b			
48.	b		26.	b	70.	a			
49.	a		27.	b	71.	a			
50	d		28.	b	72.	b			
51.	a		29.	b	73.	b			
52.	d		30.	b	74.	b			
53.	b		31.	b	75.	b			
54.	d		32.	b	76.	b			
55.	b		33.	a	77.	b			
56.	a		34.	b	78.	b			
57.	c		35.	a	79.	a			
58.	d		36.	b	80.	b			
59.	b		37.	b	81.	b			
60.	c		38.	b	82.	b			
61.	a		39.	b	83.	a			
62.	d		40.	b	84.	b			
			41.	b	85.	a			
			42.	a	86.	b			

Answer Key #2

CHAPTER ONE

Roots, Prefixes, Suffixes

The words provided are examples only; other correct answers are possible.

Section 1

1. extraterrestrial
2. anthropology
3. prescription
4. veracity
5. mission
6. reopen
7. progenitor
8. heterogeneous
9. encyclopedia
10. eulogize

Section 2

11. malady
12. postscript
13. promote
14. chronology
15. amoral
16. hyperactive
17. error
18. peripheral
19. finality
20. disentangle

Section 3

21. abnormal
22. being
23. foreboding
24. vibrant
25. pediatrics
26. dissect
27. comparable
28. auditorium
29. pugnacious
30. omnibus

Section 4

31. amiable
32. biannual
33. collusion
34. boyish
35. diaphanous
36. scientific
37. circumscribe
38. antagonist
39. egress
40. magnificent

Section 5

41. intravenous
42. convert
43. monarch
44. admit
45. interlude
46. diminish
47. suppress
48. transport
49. perceive
50. miscellaneous

Section 6

51. pedestrian
52. infrastructure
53. hydrant
54. inarticulate
55. antecedent
56. premonition
57. degenerate
58. homogeneous
59. amorphous
60. autobiography

Section 7

61. snobbery
62. recipient
63. solution
64. attractive
65. dangerous
66. transportation
67. projection
68. abduct
69. exist
70. metamorphosis

Section 8

71. visionary
72. interrogate
73. noxious
74. fidelity
75. jurisdiction
76. jury
77. transferring
78. increase
79. pyre
80. accept

Section 9

81. ambiguous
82. benefit
83. freedom
84. surface
85. immerse
86. exodus
87. alias
88. circumstance
89. bibliophile
90. polysyllabic

Section 10

91. oblique
92. neonatal
93. pension
94. manual
95. hypodermic
96. identity
97. genesis
98. pandemic
99. formulate
100. paraphrase

Section 11

101. unable
102. manly
103. spheroid
104. alcoholism
105. operate
106. dedicate
107. dynamic
108. feminine
109. epitaph
110. licit

Section 12

111. illuminate
112. philosophy
113. benefit
114. apostasy
115. exhume
116. primal
117. lucid
118. assume
119. lavage
120. placate

Confusing Words Matching Columns synonym answers

Section 1

1. precedence (a noun)
2. banality
3. ancestor
4. survey
5. encroach
6. partisan
7. review
8. violate
9. evil
10. coterie

Section 2

11. encounter
12. essential
13. fervor
14. spin
15. obsession
16. progress
17. ricochet
18. spiral
19. fleeting look
20. compulsory

Section 3

21. aggregate
22. separate from
23. harass
24. conjugal
25. secure
26. how much, how large

27. to sue
28. warlike
29. promise solemnly
30. also

Section 4

31. willingly take in
32. (a pronoun)
33. inferred
34. otherwise, elsewhere
35. additionally
36. supplement
37. otherwise
38. praise
39. clear
40. one of a number of things

Section 5

41. transport
42. power
43. depart
44. acquire
45. antedate
46. lay
47. relocate in
48. start, continue
49. rest
50. possibility

Section 6

51. main or important
52. assertion of an untruth
53. notable
54. basic truth, rule, law
55. number
56. evoke (as a verb)
57. candid
58. matters of degree

59. criminal (as an adjective)
60. put

Section 7

61. measured time
62. recurring
63. assets
64. hinted at
65. in addition
66. reluctant
67. occupied by Congress
68. unbroken
69. false perception
70. opposite position

Section 8

71. work experience
72. outer garment, proceeding in court
73. grinds prescription lenses
74. holding a lease
75. start again
76. a machine (a noun)
77. retinue
78. smaller
79. to construct (a verb)
80. examines eyes for defects

CHAPTER 3

Antonym Matching Columns

The words provided are examples only; other correct answers are possible.

Section 1

1. believer
2. satisfy
3. favoritism
4. self-govern-ing
5. cheerful
6. confuse
7. frankness
8. inequality
9. changeable
10. extravagant

Section 2

11. cranky
12. ease
13. hold
14. transitory
15. censure
16. optimistic
17. agreeable
18. foolish
19. rustic
20. separate

Section Three

21. talkative
22. abrade
23. insupportable
24. beginner
25. comprehensive
26. shapeless
27. ambivalent
28. overweight
29. integrity
30. wrong

113 ©

Bibliography

The American Heritage Desk Dictionary. Boston: Houghton Mifflin Co.: 2013.

Berry, Thomas Elliott. *The Most Common Mistakes in English Usage.* New York: McGraw-Hill, Inc., 2012.

Brittain Robert. *A Pocket Guide to Correct Punctuation.* 2d ed. Hauppauge, NY: Barron's Educational Series, 1990.

Brownstein Samuel, et al. *A Pocket Guide to Vocabulary.* 4th ed. Hauppauge, NY: Barron's Educational Series, 2004.

Brusaw, Charles. *The Business Writer's Handbook.* NY: St. Martin's Press, 2009.

Chapman, Robert, ed. *Roget's International Thesaurus.* 6th ed. New York: HarperCollins, Inc., n.d.

Goldstein, Norm, ed. *The Associated Press Stylebook and Libel Manual.* Reading, MA: Addison-Wesley Publishing Co., Inc., 1998.

Hacker, Diana. *The Writer's Reference.* 6th ed. New York: Bedford Books. n.d.

Hook, J.N. *The Appropriate Word.* Reading, MA: Addison-Wesley Publishing Co., Inc., n.d.

Le Pan, Don. *The Broadview Book of Common Errors in English.* 5th ed. Lewiston, NY: Broadview Press, n.d.

The Paragon House Spelling Dictionary. New York: Paragon House, 1993.

Paxson, William C. *The New American Dictionary of Confusing Words.* NY: Signet, 1990.

The Random House Thesaurus, College Edition. NY: Random House

Robinson, Adam, et al. *The Princeton Review Word Smart II.* New York: Villard Books, 2001.

Sabin, William A. *The Gregg Reference Manual.* 11th ed. Westerville, OH: Glencoe, n.d.

Shertzer, Margaret D. *The Elements of Grammar.* NY: Macmillan Publishing Co., 1986.

U.S. Government Printing Office. *A Manual of Style.* NY: Grammercy Publishing Co., Inc., n.d.

Webster's Legal Speller. Springfield, MA: Merriam-Webster, Inc., 1978.

Webster's New World Dictionary of Eponyms. NY: Simon & Schuster, 1990.

****Pedagogically sound covering a wealth of material
with facts, tips, information.   Time-Tested, Proven
In the Classroom and Independent Study****

The world's largest library of *court reporter training, *private tutoring, *career coaching, *test prep!

Complete NCRA and State RPR, RDR, CSR WKT Test Prep Textbook, 6th Edition, Updated/Revised

2015 Sixth Edition *Textbook*: Only textbook on the market! Latin, legal, court terms; detailed grammar, punctuation; vocabulary; medical; Expanded **Test-Taking Tips; **Additional Focus Tips; ** Updated/Expanded Computer Terminology, **Technology, **Advisory Opinions, **Ethics

Workbook follows the *Complete WKT Text*: testing resource with Latin, legal, court terms; grammar; vocabulary; medical; computer sections -- approximately 2,002 practice test questions

Companion Workbook Study Guide follows the *Workbook*, cross-referencing each word, showing where and how words are used. Learn why an answer is correct, incorrect, or the distracting answer

** "Test Prep Set" – four-volume set – is CRRbooks.com's bestseller consisting of the *Complete WKT Textbook, Workbook, Companion Study Guide,* and *Realtime Vocabulary Workbook* **

Vastly improve skills for greater career opportunities with CART Captioning and court reporting.

---

*Learn *How* to Test. ** Pass the first time!*

Join the thousands of students, novice and long-time professionals who have discovered:
- The highest-result NCRA and State Test Prep Textbook and Workbooks for testing success;
- Affordable tutoring and confidential one-on-one private coaching for your accelerated progress;
- Simple time-management and organized motivational skills to keep you moving forward.

Are you struggling with tests, motivation, personal challenges, focus, and/or speedbuilding?

Veteran court reporter, Monette Benoit, multiple-title author of books and test prep for the CART Captioning and reporting industry helps clients achieve at higher levels. Build new strengths in testing, focus, and speedbuilding. Email Monette@CRRbooks.com about tutoring, coaching packages.

Nationally known as the *Court Reporting Whisperer*, Monette provides tutoring and career coaching.

Get the latest tips and advice from www.monettebenoit.com and www.CRRbooks.com
"Monette's Musings" contains information for busy professionals and students.

NEW: RealTime Dictionary Builder, www.realtimedictionarybuilder.com
Championed by Kathy DiSanti DiLorenzo, RDR-CRR-CBC, and many others.

As a student, I felt inclined to study this material as I did academic tests. Much of the material reviewed appeared on the exam. **This text is a wonderful tool** that should be utilized by students and reporters everywhere as an aid in passing written tests.   – Laura Ballard, RPR, CSR – Ex-Student

Having been a captioner and out of reporting and testing arenas, I knew I would cram for the NCRA RDR, Registered Diplomate Reporter, exam. I chose **this textbook** and the REALTIME Vocabulary Workbook to bring myself up to date – and how out of date I was! **These books have excellent study material for the CSR, RPR, and RMR.** I received my RDR results. Thanks, Monette!   – Kathy DiSanti DiLorenzo, *RDR-CRR-CBC*

To join our successful ranks, go to: www.CRRbooks.com
